AF413163

Things That Contaminate Your Faith

The Series

The power of **Faith** is to turn your situation to your advantage. But, none of this can take place, if you're not in **Faith.**

Inspiring You To Press Forward, By **Faith.**

Minister Bernard Marrow

ByFaithWeGood
"For We Walk By Faith, Not By Sight"
2 Corinthians 5:7 KJV

BFWG Ministry Inc.

Table of
Contents

Acknowledgments

First giving honor to God who is truly the head of my life. Who is my all in all! God has been with me every step of the way. Without Him, I am nothing.

I thank God for my wife Vanessa who supports me 100%! And for my family, my mom, sisters, nieces, and nephews who are the inspiration that help keep me focused.

A special thank you and acknowledgement to Pastor Tahleen "Toi" Dailey, the founder and CEO of Purpose Kingdom Network (PKN), as well as to all my PKN family!

About This Book

Reading this book, you'll be empowered to know what not to allow to take root in your life. When it comes to your feelings and emotions, day-to-day struggles and challenges, you're about to find out why you should never allow your faith to be contaminated. This book is going to inspire you with the importance of maintaining your faith in God, His Word, plan, and purpose for your life in order to be in alignment with His will.

A word from
The Author

Family, I am so grateful for the call and purpose with which God has favored my life. As with all of Christ's ambassadors, He has called me to inspire and nourish your faith, connecting you with our Creator—who is so invested in you and loves you without limits—and the amazing future He has planned for you. It's having strong radical faith in God and His Word that will produce the manifestation of what He declared and promised in His Word. Part of my assignment is to help you be the greatest person of faith God created you to be, flowing in your fullest potential. I want to help you glorify God through the gifts He's given you, with the light of Christ shining through you on those who've been living in darkness.

We're created with the responsibility to glorify God in the way we live, how we flow, and what we produce (give birth to) in the earth. God created you to prosper, to be victorious, to succeed in all you do, to be the salt and the light in the earth!

The theme scripture for this series is:

Romans 1:16-17 KJV
"For I am not ashamed of the gospel of Christ: for it is the power of God unto salvation to every one that believeth; to the Jew first, and also to the Greek. For therein is the righteousness of God revealed from faith to faith: as it is written, The just shall live by faith."

We go from faith to faith.

When it comes to the Kingdom of God, you have to function by faith. As members of the Kingdom of God, we are never ashamed but always stand firm on the Word of the Lord.

Family, let's come together and press forward by faith!

PART 1

FEAR, PRESSURE, WORRYING

God takes us from faith to faith. God wants to get His principles, His Kingdom established in the earth. And He chose us to do it. The church is the highest authority in the earth. The church can do things on a level that the world doesn't know anything about.

Romans 1:16-17 KJV
"For I am not ashamed of the gospel of Christ: for it is the power of God unto salvation to every one that believeth; to the Jew first, and also to the Greek. For therein is the righteousness of God revealed from faith to faith: as it is written, The just shall live by faith."

We go from faith to faith. When it comes to the Kingdom of God, you have to function by faith. The power of faith is to turn your situation to your advantage. But none of this can take place if you're not acting in faith. There are things and ways about us that can contaminate our faith, and make us ineffective for God, ourselves, and others. There are things and ways about us that we allow at times to contaminate our faith and negatively affect what we believe.

To be contaminated is:
• having been made impure by exposure to something or a polluting substance.
• to infect or be infected by contact or association.
• to make something or someone unfit for use (not being pure to be used by God) by adding something harmful or unpleasant.

In this Part 1, Family, let's begin by seeing how fear can contaminate our faith.

FEAR

Definition: An unpleasant emotion caused by the belief that someone or something is dangerous, likely to cause pain, or be a threat.

All of us have fears of some kind. Maybe you are afraid of losing your job, losing your finances, or losing a loved one that you have depended on for affection and acceptance. Maybe you have fears about loneliness, fears about being accepted by others, fears about failure, fears about rejection. Fears for your children, fears about your relationships, or fears of facing tomorrow. Sometimes our young people have fears of going to school, fears of being bullied, fears of being talked about, fears of not being accepted, or fears of traveling alone. Whatever your fear may be, you have uttered the words, "I am afraid," at one time or another, privately or publicly. This feeling of fear has a powerful influence on how we think and act.

How do you react when gripped by fear?

We all are vulnerable to fear. How we react or manage it when it grips our soul is very important. If our reaction is unbiblical and unbecoming, allowing fear to conquer our soul and our faith, we may become bound by fear. Fear can cause us to isolate ourselves and withdraw ourselves emotionally, unable to enjoy the life God has given us the spirit of fear; but of power, and of love, and of a sound mind" (KJV).

By faith, you can break out of fear in Jesus' Mighty Name and walk in Victory!

Something else that can contaminate your faith is **Pressure.**

PRESSURE

Definition: the use of persuasion, influence, or intimidation to make someone do something.

Another way the enemy tries to come at you is by pressuring you. Pressuring you to stay in your feelings, pressuring you to give up, pressuring you to give into lust, pressuring you to hang around certain people (because if you don't, then you're not cool or won't be accepted).

The enemy will try to pressure you to feel like you're not loved or have to fit in instead of loving yourself and being confident about who God created you to be. People often manipulate other people because they're not confident in who they are. The enemy will try to pressure you through your peers, trying to trick you into smoking again, drinking again, hanging out in certain areas again. He will pressure you into feeling as though you can't be great being who God created you to be. He will say you can't be successful, and the ideas and creativity God has downloaded into you won't work.

But the devil is a liar!

You're created to live by faith under God's grace, not pressure from the enemy. Your body and organs don't function properly when you operate under pressure. Your body is always aching and painful. You feel off-balance or unwell. Being fearful and under pressure distracts you from what God wants to reveal to you and where God wants to take you.

You have to function by faith and not by fear or as one under pressure.

When the enemy tries to put pressure on you, put the pressure back on him with the Word of God. Don't be fearful. Remain strong in your faith, in Jesus' Mighty Name!

Another thing that can contaminate your faith is **Worry.**

WORRY

Definition: *To give way to anxiety or unease; allow one's mind to dwell on difficulties or troubles; causing anxiety about actual or potential problems; alarming.*

To have anxiety is to frequently have intense, excessive and persistent worry and fear about everyday situations. Anxiety is an emotion characterized by feelings of tension, worried thoughts, and physical changes like increased blood pressure. People with anxiety disorders usually have recurring intrusive thoughts or concerns. They may avoid certain situations out of worry.

Worrying is a waste of time! It can be labeled as a sin, because worrying shows lack of faith in God. However, it's comforting to know that the same God who is in control of the good times of life is also in control of the bad times.

1 Peter 5:7 KJV

"Casting all your care upon him; for he careth for you."
God cares about everything that concerns you! God sees, He knows, and He'll never leave you hanging. Get excited, because with God every situation is always working for your good (Romans 8:28)!

Psalm 55:2 KJV
"Cast thy burden upon the LORD, and he shall sustain thee: he shall never suffer the righteous to be moved."

This is the grace and love of God towards us. Don't try to carry your burdens by yourself. Give them to the Lord whose yoke is easy and burden is light! Our worries weigh us down and do us no good. Give your worries all over to God, because He can handle the weight of all your worries and your fears. Because God's Spirit lives within us, we can be strong and courageous. Fear, worrying, and being under pressure contaminate faith. You can't allow worry, fear, or pressure to destroy and contaminate you and your faith. By faith, you have the power through Jesus Christ to break out of fearing, being under pressure, and worrying!

#ByFaithWeGood

PART 2

NEGATIVE THOUGHTS, WRONGFUL SPEAKING

Recap:
God takes us from faith to faith. God wants to get His principles, His Kingdom established in the earth. And He chose us to do it. The church is the highest authority in the earth. The church can do things on a level that the world doesn't know anything about.

Romans 1:16-17 KJV
"For I am not ashamed of the gospel of Christ: for it is the power of God unto salvation to every one that believeth; to the Jew first, and also to the Greek. For therein is the righteousness of God revealed from faith to faith: as it is written, The just shall live by faith."

We go from faith to faith. You have to function by faith in the Kingdom of God. The power of faith is to turn your situation to your advantage. This cannot take place if you're not acting in faith. There are things that can contaminate our faith, and make us ineffective for God, ourselves, and others. There are ways about us that we allow at times to contaminate our faith and negatively affect what we believe.

To be contaminated is:
- having been made impure by exposure to something or a polluting-substance.
- to infect or be infected by contact or association.
- to make something or someone unfit for use (not being pure to be used by God) by adding something harmful or unpleasant.

In Part 1, we found out how **Fear, Pressure,** and **Worry** can contaminate your faith.

In Part 2, we're going to find out what else can contaminate your faith, starting with **Negative Thoughts.**

NEGATIVE THOUGHTS

Romans 12:2 KJV
"And be not conformed to this world: but be ye transformed by the renewing of your mind, that ye may prove what is that good, and acceptable, and perfect, will of God."

Transformation and remaining strong in faith comes when you renew your mind. You are equipped, blessed, talented, and empowered. Because of that, you can be focused, bold, and confident. But it is up to you to bring it out.

How do you do this?

We find out in the Bible that God transforms you into a new person by changing the way you think. Negative thoughts make you believe that things will never change, that you are destined for misery for the rest of your life, and that being alive may not be worth it. When you let go of small thinking—when you stop limiting God—you open up your life to your dreams and the fullness of God's blessings. You find yourself no longer conforming to the pattern of the world but to the will of God. Our behavior will change when our thinking changes.

Hebrews 12:1-2 KJV
"Wherefore seeing we also are compassed about with so great a cloud of witnesses, let us lay aside every weight, and the sin which doth so easily beset us, and let us run with patience the race that is set before us, Looking unto Jesus the author and finisher of our faith; who for the joy that was set before him endured the cross, despising the shame, and is set down at the right hand of the throne of God."

We need to learn, and always remember, to stay focused and look to Jesus.

Hebrews 12 is an exhortation to be constant and persevere. The example of persevering obedience and faith in Christ is set forth. The race set before the Hebrews, wherein they must either win the crown of glory or have everlasting misery for their portion is the same race set before us.

Think of your mind as a GARDEN, and your thoughts are the SEEDS. You can grow FLOWERS, or you can grow WEEDS. Your mind will always believe everything you tell it. Our responsibility, Family, is to:

FEED YOUR MIND with FAITH! (Believing)

FEED YOUR MIND with TRUTH! (The Word of God)

FEED YOUR MIND with LOVE! (Who God is)

When you think things are never going to change and will never get better, that kind of thinking determines your course of action. You'll put limitations on yourself when there is no limit to how far God can take you! Greater is always ahead of you!

Proverbs 23:7 KJV
"For as he thinketh in his heart, so is he…"

What is in you will always come out of you. To be strong in faith, you have to make sure your thoughts and heart are pure. God wants to equip and empower you for your next level. Let God recharge, refresh, renew, and restore you by getting rid of those defeating, negative thoughts!

What else can contaminate your faith?

WRONGFUL SPEAKING

We need to stop speaking defeat in our lives. I believe God is tired of His children saying, "I don't know what I'm going to do," when problems come our way. God wants you to stop speaking defeat in your life. He wants you to know that there is power in your mouth. There's power in what you say!

Proverbs 18:21 KJV
"Death and life are in the power of the tongue: and they that love it shall eat the fruit thereof."

The power of life and death is in what you say! Through Jesus Christ, you have the power and authority by faith to speak over and change what takes place in your environment. You have the power to take control over what's happening around you! Because God is for us, NOTHING can come against us. Words are seeds. The words we speak are creative. Our words give birth and bring into existence what is not.

By faith, our words can bring forth breakthroughs. Our words can turn impossibilities into possibilities (Mark 11:23). We can speak with the authority we have through Jesus Christ!

When we speak wrongfully, we find ourselves saying things that we don't normally say. We speak curses over our lives instead of the Word of God. We say, "I'm sick," and "I'm tired," and leave it there instead of speaking, "By the stripes of Jesus I am healed" (Isaiah 53:5) and "In my weakness, His strength is made perfect" (2 Corinthians 12:9). We'll curse someone out and give them a piece of our mind, instead of praying for them like God's Word says: "Pray for them which despitefully use you" (Luke 6:28 KJV).

Some people don't have any mind left, because of what they allowed themselves to get caught up in. If you have been saved, you are a child of God, and with that you have the mind of Christ. When you give your mind up to the enemy and this world, you have allowed something to contaminate what you believe. You have given up your faith.

These things and others contaminate our faith. They cause our faith to weaken. Speaking in a way that doesn't add value to our lives, our purpose, and our environment, as well as the people around us, contaminates our faith. Yet we wonder why things are not working for us.

Why haven't you rebuked the spirit of sickness or any other toxic, negative, malicious spirit from your midst?

We wonder why prayers aren't answered or are hindered. It is because we're not speaking correctly. Without realizing it, you have taken ownership of things, bad habits, and spirits that God did not send to you. You've allowed these things to come in and contaminate your very being, causing you to be "sick," unable to believe. These block you from acting on or even hearing the promises of God. Instead of having the faith to manifest what God wants to do in your life and not what the world implements, you fall prey to the world's influence.

Speaking incorrectly is a barrier. Not speaking the way God created you to speak is a blessing blocker. Your faith has been contaminated. To speak wrongfully is to speak against God's will. It is to speak in a way that tears down, instead of building up. It is a way that wounds and doesn't heal!

I encourage you, Family, to decontaminate your faith by speaking the Word of the Lord over yourself.

Say, "I'm the head, and not the tail!"

"I'm above only and not beneath!"

"I'm a lender and not a borrower!"
"I'm more than a conqueror through Jesus Christ who loves me at all times!"

"I'm an overcomer!"

"I'm victorious!"

"I shall never lose but shall always win!"

"I shall never fail but shall always succeed!"

"I will not be distracted!"

"I will not be held back!"

"I will not drown in my feelings or emotions!"

"I will not give in to any lustful or fleshly desires!"

"I'm gonna stay focused, walking by faith and not by sight or how I feel!"

#ByFaithWeGood

PART 3

BITTERNESS

Recap:
God takes us from faith to faith. God wants to get His principles, His Kingdom established in the earth. And He chose us to do it. The church is the highest authority in the earth. The church can do things on a level that the world doesn't know anything about.

Romans 1:16-17 KJV

"For I am not ashamed of the gospel of Christ: for it is the power of God unto salvation to every one that believeth; to the Jew first, and also to the Greek. For therein is the righteousness of God revealed from faith to faith: as it is written, The just shall live by faith."

We go from faith to faith. You have to function by faith in the Kingdom of God. The power of faith is to turn your situation to your advantage. This cannot take place if you're not acting in faith. There are things that can contaminate our faith, and make us ineffective for God, ourselves, and others. There are ways about us that we allow at times to contaminate our faith and negatively affect what we believe.
To be contaminated is:

- having been made impure by exposure to something or a polluting substance.
- to infect or be infected by contact or association.
- to make something or someone unfit for use (not being pure to be used by God) by adding something harmful or unpleasant.

So far, Family, we have found out how fear, pressure, worry, negative thoughts, and wrongful speaking can contaminate your faith.

Family, it's so important that we not live according to our emotions, but that we live by faith according to God's Word. There are so many things and emotions that can contaminate our faith. I want to take my time going through this series so that we can learn how to remain strong in faith.

In Part 3, we're going to find out how **Bitterness** can contaminate your faith.

BITTERNESS
Definition: *Anger, disappointment, or resentment.*

When it comes to people, bitterness involves their feelings or behavior.

Being bitter can include being sad, angry, hurt, or resentful because of bad experiences or a sense of unjust treatment. Being bitter can contaminate your faith! Another way to describe being bitter is being in your feelings. If you're in your feelings, you're not in faith. When you're not in faith, you're not covered!

In addition to God's grace, mercy, and favor, it takes faith to produce the results of God's character and promises. Being bitter is not good, Family. Bitterness causes symptoms of trauma like sleeplessness, fatigue, and stress. In the long term, it can also lead to low self-confidence, negative personalities, and an inability to have healthy relationships!

We're gonna get into Ruth 1 and 2 to see the importance of making sure we stay strong in faith and remain committed and devoted to God.

Ruth 1:1-22 NLT

"In the days when the judges ruled in Israel, a severe famine came upon the land. So a man from Bethlehem in Judah left his home and went to live in the country of Moab, taking his wife and two sons with him. The man's name was Elimelech, and his wife was Naomi. Their two sons were Mahlon and Kilion. They were Ephrathites from Bethlehem in the land of Judah. And when they reached Moab, they settled there.

"Then Elimelech died, and Naomi was left with her two sons. The two sons married Moabite women. One married a woman named Orpah, and the other a woman named Ruth. But about ten years later, both Mahlon and Kilion died. This left Naomi alone, without her two sons or her husband.

"Then Naomi heard in Moab that the Lord had blessed his people in Judah by giving them good crops again. So Naomi and her daughters-in-law got ready to leave Moab to return to her homeland. With her two daughters-in-law she set out from the place where she had been living, and they took the road that would lead them back to Judah.

"But on the way, Naomi said to her two daughters-in-law, 'Go back to your mothers' homes. And may the Lord reward you for your kindness to your husbands and to me. May the Lord bless you with the security of another marriage.' Then she kissed them good-bye, and they all broke down and wept.

"'No,' they said. 'We want to go with you to your people.'

"But Naomi replied, 'Why should you go on with me? Can I still give birth to other sons who could grow up to be your husbands? No, my daughters, return to your parents' homes, for I am too old to marry again. And even if it were possible, and I were to get married tonight and bear sons, then what? Would you wait for them to grow up and refuse to marry someone else? No, of course not, my daughters! Things are far more bitter for me than for you, because the Lord himself has raised his fist against me.'

"And again they wept together, and Orpah kissed her mother-in-law good-bye. But Ruth clung tightly to Naomi. 'Look,' Naomi said to her, 'your sister-in-law has gone back to her people and to her gods. You should do the same.'

"But Ruth replied, 'Don't ask me to leave you and turn back. Wherever you go, I will go; wherever you live, I will live. Your people will be my people, and your God will be my God. Wherever you die, I will die, and there I will be buried. May the Lord punish me severely if I allow anything but death to separate us!' When Naomi saw that Ruth was determined to go with her, she said nothing more.

"So the two of them continued on their journey. When they came to Bethlehem, the entire town was excited by their arrival. 'Is it really Naomi?' the women asked.

"'Don't call me Naomi,' she responded. 'Instead, call me Mara, for the Almighty has made life very bitter for me. I went away full, but the Lord has brought me home empty. Why call me Naomi when the Lord has caused me to suffer and the Almighty has sent such tragedy upon me?'

"So Naomi returned from Moab, accompanied by her daughter-in-law Ruth, the young Moabite woman. They arrived in Bethlehem in late spring, at the beginning of the barley harvest."

Ruth was the daughter-in-law of Naomi. When Naomi's husband and sons died, she set out to Judah along with her daughters-in-law, Ruth and Orpah. While on the journey, Naomi insisted that her daughters-in-law go back to their country. Orpah went back, but Ruth clung to Naomi. Ruth clung to Naomi, stating that she would go with Naomi and not leave her.

It is in some of the most unique cases where a God-honoring caregiver is determined to take care of the one in need although the one in need insists otherwise. I believe Ruth followed the promptings of God to follow Naomi, all while trusting Him through the unknown. Ruth helped care for Naomi, even though Naomi insisted Ruth just take care of herself. Ruth faithfully exhibited resilience as she cared for her mother-in-law during many challenges. Ruth's resilience in sowing God-honoring seeds while caring for her mother-in-law, even when change seemed far off, produced a harvest in her life that most likely exceeded her expectations.

If you desire to walk in the supernatural with God, if you desire to align yourself and your life with God, there will be a moment in which you must make the same choice Ruth made. Ruth was willing to give up everything. She left her family behind. She left her culture and traditions behind. She left her home behind. She abandoned everything that the outside world valued. Ruth abandoned going back to her own homeland all for the sake of following the way of God.

As she said to Naomi, "For whither thou goest, I will go; and where thou lodgest, I will lodge: thy people shall be my people, and thy God my God" (Ruth 1:16 KJV).

Not only did she love her mother-in-law with a deep and tender love, but she confessed her inner longing to unite with the people of Israel and to forsake all so that she might follow God!

Ruth 1:19-21 NLT
"So the two of them continued on their journey. When they came to Bethlehem, the entire town was excited by their arrival. 'Is it really Naomi?' the women asked.
"'Don't call me Naomi,' she responded. 'Instead, call me Mara, for the Almighty has made life very bitter for me. I went away full, but the Lord has brought me home empty. Why call me Naomi when the Lord has caused me to suffer and the Almighty has sent such tragedy upon me?'

There's a lesson here. When you have decided that God is against you, you exaggerate your hopelessness. You can become so bitter that you can't see the rays of light peeking around the clouds.

It was God who broke the famine and opened the way home for them (Ruth 1:6). It was God who preserved a kinsman (Boaz) to continue Naomi's line (Ruth 2:20). And it was God who constrained Ruth to stay with Naomi.

But Naomi is so embittered by God's hard providence that she can't see His mercy and plan at work in her life.

There's a revelation here. Naomi is embittered by God's hard providence.

The word **Providence** means "providing protective spiritual care; the protective care of God, a spiritual power."

This is another reason why you can't allow your faith to be contaminated, Family! God may allow some things to take place in your life, but He is protecting you at the same time!

Naomi didn't realize that, in the midst of what was happening, God was still taking care of her, and He had chosen Ruth as the vessel to work through.

I admit, Naomi endured a hard hit. She lost her husband and both her sons. That's not something to take lightly. But she allowed herself to become so bitter that she couldn't see the purpose in God's plan. Naomi allowed bitterness to contaminate her faith. She had no desire to live happily again. She had no hope, and she didn't care about anything that was in store for them. How many of you can thank God today, in spite of what has happened in your life? Are you grateful that God connected you with people who remained strong and stuck by you, who helped you break out of your feelings when necessary?

Thank God that those who He connected you with didn't let you sink. They didn't let you give up. They didn't let you give in. Instead they helped you make the decision to say, "I'm breaking out of how I feel! I'm getting my faith back! And I'm sticking with Jesus!" We have to remain strong in faith. Some people haven't even taken a hard hit like

Naomi, yet they allow bitterness to consume them.

Some people are just bitter because of the way they grew up.

Some people are just bitter because of what other people have.

Some people are just bitter because everything is not all about them.

Some people are just bitter because somebody was talking about them.

Let them talk! You keep moving towards what God has in store for you and what He has called you to do.

Some people are just bitter because they have nothing better to do.

Get with God and He'll give you something to do!

Family, don't allow your faith to be contaminated by bitterness. Don't allow yourself to be trapped in bitterness, in your feelings.

Ruth 1:19-21 NLT
"So the two of them continued on their journey. When they came to Bethlehem, the entire town was excited by their arrival. 'Is it really Naomi?' the women asked.
"'Don't call me Naomi,' she responded. 'Instead, call me Mara, for the Almighty has made life very bitter for me. I went away full, but the Lord has brought me home empty. Why call me Naomi when the Lord has caused me to suffer and the Almighty has sent such tragedy upon me?'

Naomi left Bethlehem when a severe famine took place and returned to Bethlehem at harvest. She left Judah "full and pleasant" and returned "bitter" (as Mara). Ruth "returned" with her. Although she was not an Israelite by birth, she was now one as she clung to her mother-in-law Naomi and God.

Ruth is a hint of hope, as one who "comes back" to where she was never thought to belong. Ruth, who was not an Israelite but a Moabite woman, now belongs to the God of Israel in Bethlehem because of her faithfulness. She has been grafted into God's family. It is important to recognize and understand the current phase of our life. This will change our perspective.

Here, Naomi was at the highest level of frustration. Note that it was at the beginning of the harvest. The word to us today is, "The extremity of our trials is the beginning of our deliverance."

Family, let's get into Ruth 2.

Ruth 2:12 NLT

"'May the Lord, the God of Israel, under whose wings you have come to take refuge, reward you fully for what you have done.'"

Ruth goes to glean barley from the field of Boaz, Naomi's wealthy kinsman. Boaz arrives from Bethlehem, sees the reapers in his field and blesses them. Then he sees Ruth, who is not an Israelite but a Moabite, and he asks his servant who she is. Boaz is a redeemer of those who were poor, lost, and overlooked, and he takes special notice of Ruth.

As a poor foreigner, widow, and caretaker for her mother-in-law, Ruth would have been considered one of the lowest members of any society. Yet this high-ranking man of God stooped down and noticed her. Boaz promised her protection, food, drink, and refuge while showing her kindness and grace. Her exemplary character went before her, and Boaz blessed her, asking God to repay her and reward her fully for her actions and faithfulness.

When we accept Jesus as our Lord and Savior, He becomes our redeemer. He has looked down upon our pitiful status and shown us mercy and kindness that we do not deserve, even submitting Himself to death on the cross for our sake. Then He rose with all power! What an amazing Savior we have, and what lengths He is willing to go for our benefit. Take a moment and thank God for His amazing love, kindness, grace, and mercy towards you.

By following her heart and doing what she knew was right, Ruth went from being a foreigner to being someone who was respected, blessed, and honored. Ruth knew the value of family and relationships, and her loyalty paid off. Our actions speak louder than our words, even when we don't know people are watching. Ruth's protection, blessings, and marriage to Boaz were a direct result of her faithfulness to God. Ruth could have been bitter as well. She could have been caught up in her feelings. She could have followed Naomi's instructions to leave her and go another way.

I agree, loss is never easy. Losing loved ones hurts. It's difficult to understand. At times, you may even feel as though you can't go on without them. It's okay to have your moments to grieve and heal, but through it all we have to make the decision to stay with God. We must remain strong in faith. Don't allow the enemy to keep you trapped in your feelings. Don't allow the enemy to cause you to be bitter and to stay there. In order for our faith to remain uncontaminated, Family, we've got to learn how to bounce back from what we've gone through! In times when we may be weak or hurting, we need to be with those to whom God has and will connect us, who can remain strong and remind us of the great only true Living God that we serve: our Lord and Savior Jesus Christ.

In spite of our loss, in spite of our hurts, in spite of shame and times of loneliness, God remains the same. He never leaves nor forsakes you. He never abandons you. God stays with you every step of the way, protecting, providing for, and healing you. Like Ruth, even in the midst of uncertainty, you can stay committed to God and trust how He's leading you. God still has a greater plan for your life that involves prosperity, healing, deliverance, and full restoration.

Remember Ruth's words to Naomi: "For whither thou goest, I will go; and where thou lodgest, I will lodge: thy people shall be my people, and thy God my God" (Ruth 1:16 KJV).

Not only did Ruth love her mother-in-law with a deep and tender love, but she confessed her inner longing to unite with the people of Israel and to forsake all so that she might follow after God! Despite what took place, Ruth made a decision to not be bitter but to stick with God and who He connected her with. Declare today and everyday that, no matter what you go through, you're going to stay with God and remain strong in faith.

While Naomi was sad and felt broken, she was blessed to have Ruth. Naomi didn't know that she was returning with the Lord's promise. Naomi didn't know that she was still right on track with what God had planned for them. Indeed, the promise was clinging to her. Ruth was destined to carry the line of Christ, and her covenant with Naomi was the Lord's will. Out of their pain and loss, the Lord brought hope, purpose, joy, and restoration.

God brought Hope into the world through their obedient steps of faith to cling to and trust Him. Things don't always go according to our plans, but when we take heed to and follow God, we'll realize His plan is so much better than we can even imagine. Naomi and Ruth left Judah empty; when they returned to Bethlehem, it was harvest time! God's timing is perfect. Trust in the Lord, and let Him lead you.

#ByFaithWeGood

PART 4

DOUBT

Romans 1:16-17 KJV
"For I am not ashamed of the gospel of Christ: for it is the power of God unto salvation to every one that believeth; to the Jew first, and also to the Greek. For therein is the righteousness of God revealed from faith to faith: as it is written, The just shall live by faith."

We go from faith to faith.

We cannot be ashamed to love God, to serve God, to trust God, to commit our life to being in and maintaining a personal relationship with Him. You have to function by faith in the Kingdom of God.

The power of faith is to turn your situation to your advantage. This cannot take place if you're not acting in faith. There are things that can contaminate our faith, and make us ineffective for God, ourselves, and others.

There are ways about us that we allow at times to contaminate our faith and negatively affect what we believe.

Remember, to be contaminated is:

- having been made impure by exposure to something or a polluting substance.
- to infect or be infected by contact or association.
- to make something or someone unfit for use (not being pure to be used by God) by adding something harmful or unpleasant.

I know, Family, what you've just read has been in every chapter so far. That's because it's so important that we understand this, so we can live the life God created us to live fearlessly, uncontaminated, not distracted, never defeated, but always victorious.

I have some questions for you, Family.

Who and what are you connected to or associated with?

There are things and ways about us that we allow at times to contaminate our faith and negatively affect what we believe.

How you position yourself, and who and what you allow to take root in your life, will determine how you press forward. It will determine how you respond to situations and how you treat people. It will create the vibes you then implement in your family, in your community, everywhere you go, and in all that you do.

God takes us from faith to faith. God wants to get His principles, His Kingdom established in the earth. And He chose us to do it.

Let's do an assessment, Family.

What are you allowing to take root in your life that is blocking what God promised to manifest and fulfill in your life?

What is blocking what God wants to do through and for you?

What is holding you back?

Is it your feelings and emotions?

Is it something someone did to you that's causing you to hold a grudge?

What needs to happen in order for you to press forward in the direction God is leading you?

What do you need to let go of that you have been holding on to?

What needs to change in your life?

Let those questions marinate. Take time to do your assessment so that you can properly align yourself with God.

One thing that can contaminate your faith, Family, is **Doubt**.

DOUBT

Definition: To be uncertain about (something); to believe that (something) may not be true or is unlikely; to have no confidence in (someone or something).

Doubt is a lack of certainty. It is also a lack of conviction. It is not having the Holy Spirit (being baptized with and receiving the Holy Spirit) or taking heed to the leading of the Holy Spirit!

Doubt can also cause you to be fearful or afraid.

As I shared with you all in Part 1 of this series, it's not good to operate in fear because fear will cripple you, stagnate you, paralyze you, and hold you back. Fear will literally take your faith away, leave you stuck, and destroy your confidence.

Doubt does the same. Fear and doubt go hand and hand, working together to block you from the greater things that God wants you to enjoy and even establish in the earth. They can hinder you from advancing God's Kingdom in the earth!

This is why we have to go from faith to faith. Family, it is the trials and tribulations in the lives of God's children that refine our trust in God and increase our dependence upon the Lord. Our personal difficulties and everyday dangers, and our reaction to the distress and despair of others, often determine whether we hold fast to what we believe. Do we believe in Jesus Christ's sufficient strength that He freely provides and pours into us, or do we allow seeds of doubt to darken our hearts to the goodness of God?

Those of us who have a personal relationship with Jesus Christ have been through so much and seen the hand of God at work through it all. He works every situation out for our good. We should not allow ourselves to be at a place of doubt today. You have to make up your mind that you will not allow what you see to dictate what you believe. We're created to "walk by faith, not by sight" (2 Corinthians 5:7)! Despite the lies the enemy tries to throw at you, you have to stand firm on what God says in His Word.

James 1:5-8 KJV
"If any of you lack wisdom, let him ask of God, that giveth to all men

liberally, and upbraideth not; and it shall be given him. But let him ask in faith, nothing wavering. For he that wavereth is like a wave of the sea driven with the wind and tossed. For let not that man think that he shall receive any thing of the Lord. A double minded man is unstable in all his ways."

James 1:5-8 NLT
"If you need wisdom, ask our generous God, and he will give it to you. He will not rebuke you for asking. But when you ask him, be sure that your faith is in God alone. Do not waver, for a person with divided loyalty is as unsettled as a wave of the sea that is blown and tossed by the wind. Such people should not expect to receive anything from the Lord. Their loyalty is divided between God and the world, and they are unstable in everything they do."

Going to God in prayer is being fully assured that you'll get an answer. When you ask your Heavenly Father for wisdom—when you ask your Heavenly Father for whatever you need—He promises in His Word to give it to you without finding fault. God's wisdom will kick in, in every situation, even when you think you aren't prepared for particular issues and challenges. As children of God, we use God's wisdom for Kingdom purposes. We do His will, make right and better decisions, and properly manage all that we've been given. But this only happens when we are loyal and keep our faith strong in God alone. He is the only source that we need for all that we need.

All things are possible with God, and nothing is beyond His power. Having unwavering faith, you give thanks for the answer from the moment you make your request known to God, looking forward to the fulfillment with great expectation. When you stay focused and genuinely believe, you press forward knowing what you've declared and requested of God is already done in Jesus' Name. Having strong faith is necessary in order to press forward toward what God has in store for you. Unwavering faith is to count those things that are not as though they are. There is no need for God's children to be trapped in fear, weakness, poverty, or despair.

To receive from God we must believe, hold tightly to, and protect our faith without wavering. Family, in the same way that faith and fear cannot coexist, faith and doubt cannot coexist!

This leads me to this next point in God's Word: you don't want to have **Faith Without Root**.

FAITH WITHOUT ROOT

Luke 8:13 KJV
"They on the rock are they, which, when they hear, receive the word with joy; and these have no root, which for a while believe, and in time of temptation fall away."

Luke 8:13 NLT
"The seeds on the rocky soil represent those who hear the message and receive it with joy. But since they don't have deep roots, they believe for a while, then they fall away when they face temptation."

Family, God is showing us that you can have faith, and still be all over the place. You can have faith one moment and the next moment be in doubt.

In Luke 8:13, Jesus speaks of having faith without root. It is the type of faith that springs up quickly and beautifully but, because it has no depth, it weakens and fails just as quickly when temptation and trials come along.

It's one thing to have faith when you are hearing a good word from the Lord being spoken, but will you still have that same faith, when trials, temptations, and tough times come?

Jesus shows us in Luke 8:13 that faith without root exists because the soil has not been adequately prepared by digging and searching for the knowledge, guidance, and truth found in the Word of God.

That's why God tells us in Colossians 2:6-7, "As ye have therefore received Christ Jesus the Lord, so walk ye in him: Rooted and built up in him, and stablished in the faith, as ye have been taught, abounding therein with thanksgiving" (KJV).

Here Paul says it is important to have a Christ-centered life. He also shows us how to continue in the calling that you and I have over our lives.

We must be rooted in Christ.

Roots provide stability for their tree. They also gather nutrients in order for the tree to grow. Family, in order to make sure our faith is not contaminated, we have to be rooted in Jesus Christ.

How?

First, we must have a personal relationship with Jesus Christ.

Then, we have to be rooted in Jesus Christ.

How?!

We have to cultivate daily disciplines, like reading the Bible, the Word of God; praying and having a prayer life; worshiping God for who He is; and seeking God daily for knowledge, wisdom, understanding, and His instructions through the leading of the Holy Spirit.

We have a vicious enemy seeking to shipwreck our faith and draw us away from the goodness of God. The enemy's strategy is to plant seeds of doubt in the mind of all believers, so that their lives are not fruitful or honoring to the Lord. The trials and tribulations that are designed by the enemy to unsteady our faith, however, can be used as the catalyst to strengthen our trust in God, if we will but persevere in God's sufficient strength. This brings honor to our Father in heaven and an eternal reward for those that patiently endure.

We do not have the capacity to stand firm in these evil days in our own strength, but Jesus Christ has promised that His grace is sufficient. When we hold fast to the precious promises of God and remain anchored to the truth of His holy Word, we will not be tossed about like a frothy wave in a sea of doubt. Instead we will be anchored to the truth of God's sufficient grace.

Somebody ought to shout, "Devil, you can't make me doubt God, because I know too much about Him!"

"I know God as my healer!"

"I know God as my way maker!"
"I know Him as my provider!"

"I know God as my refuge and fortress, my place of safety!"

Is there somebody out there reading this that can agree with me and shout?

"Nothing can make me doubt God!"

"Because I know Him to be a very present help in times of trouble!"

"Because I know God to be a very present help at all times!"

God will help you in every financial situation.

God will help you overcome every obstacle and press through every challenge.

God will help you to be steadfast and unmovable.

Family, I want to encourage you, never doubt. Only believe!

God will always take care of you.

Family, never doubt God. Only believe!

Remain faithful to God and be strong in faith.

Because God will always take care of you.

As I've shared before in my Monday Motivational Moment, Family, you don't have to live in uncertainty, because everything God promised is guaranteed!

2 Corinthians 1:20 KJV
"For all the promises of God in him are yea, and in him Amen, unto the glory of God by us."

In this life, there are hardships, trials, and tough circumstances, but God is our faithful Father. As children of God, we have to take God at

His Word and live in the way that He created us to: by faith, no matter what comes our way. With God, our path is straight and not crooked. God gives us the strength we need to run well, pressing forward, with God holding us up so we don't stumble.

In Christ we have a life where joy and peace is our full portion, where He provides for us in every time of need. He covers us, keeping us safe from all danger seen and unseen. God's Word is true! All of God's promises are "Yes!" and "Amen!" and are guaranteed to be fulfilled in our life.

Be encouraged, Family. Press forward. God is faithful. He's perfect in all His ways. He does all things well. And He's always on time.

You don't have to live in uncertainty, because everything God promised is guaranteed.

Let Jesus lead you. Stay Focused. Always press forward by faith.

Family, never doubt God. Only believe!

#ByFaithWeGood

PART 5

DIVISION

Romans 1:16-17 KJV

"For I am not ashamed of the gospel of Christ: for it is the power of God unto salvation to every one that believeth; to the Jew first, and also to the Greek. For therein is the righteousness of God revealed from faith to faith: as it is written, The just shall live by faith."

We go from faith to faith. God takes us from faith to faith. We're created to live from Faith to Faith. From the beginning to the end, from start to finish. We cannot be ashamed to love God, to serve God, to trust God, to commit our life to being in, and maintaining a personal relationship with Him!

The power of faith is to turn your situation to your advantage. This cannot take place if you're not acting in faith. There are things that can contaminate our faith, and make us ineffective for God, ourselves, and others. There are ways about us that we allow at times to contaminate our faith and negatively affect what we believe.

In this Part 5, we're gonna get into something else that can contaminate your faith, and that's **Division**.

DIVISION

Definition: The action of separating something into parts or the process of being separated; disagreement between two or more groups, typically producing tension or hostility.

Family, we're not created to be divided; we're created to be unified. Why? Because there's power in unity.

We're not in alignment with God when divided. We're not effective in our assignments or walking in our purpose when divided. We can block many blessings and even get in the way instead of following the way of God when divided. Division contaminates our faith, because part of living by faith is to show forth what we believe by our actions.

If we're divided, it's possible we're not supporting each other in the way we're supposed to. We're not showing and sowing in love the way we're supposed to. We're not looking out for or looking after or checking up on each other in the way we're supposed to. If none of this is taking place, we're definitely not praying for and encouraging each other through God's Word in the way we're supposed to.

Ephesians 2:14-16 NLT

"For Christ himself has brought peace to us. He united Jews and Gentiles into one people when, in his own body on the cross, he broke down the wall of hostility that separated us. He did this by ending the system of law with its commandments and regulations. He made peace between Jews and Gentiles by creating in himself one new people from the two groups. Together as one body, Christ reconciled both groups to God by means of his death on the cross, and our hostility toward each other was put to death."

Ephesians 4:5-13 KJV

"One Lord, one faith, one baptism, One God and Father of all, who is above all, and through all, and in you all. But unto every one of us is given grace according to the measure of the gift of Christ. Wherefore he saith, When he ascended up on high, he led captivity captive, and gave gifts unto men. (Now that he ascended, what is it but that he also descended first into the lower parts of the earth? He that descended is the same also that ascended up far above all heavens, that he might fill all things.) And he gave some, apostles; and some, prophets; and some, evangelists; and some, pastors and teachers; For the perfecting of the saints, for the work of the ministry, for the edifying of the body of Christ: Till we all come in the unity of the faith, and of the knowledge of the Son of God, unto a perfect man, unto the measure of the stature of the fulness of Christ:"

Unity can be defined as any group of people who are characterized by a shared purpose, vision, or direction. It's not about being the exact same but about advancing toward the same goal.

Think about a football team. There are different positions on the field. Each position has different skill sets, roles, and responsibilities. But all players on the team march toward the same end-zone because their goal is the same.

We have all heard the phrase "divide and conquer." In war, this strategy forces the enemy to divide their defenses, which leaves them vulnerable. Satan uses these same tactics against the body of Christ. He seeks to divide and conquer, because he knows that a disunited church is weak. This is why we're created to be unified.

The enemy knows how powerful we are when we're unified, so he will try to cause division, to come at you. There are people you're attached to, and it's because of their prayers that you're still standing. They are people who genuinely love and care about you. They check up on you and want to see you succeed. They help you "be strong in the Lord, and in the power of his might" (Ephesians 6:10 KJV).

This doesn't mean you're weak when you're by yourself, Family. This just means there are people God strategically assigned to you. That's why the enemy will try to divide: he wants to back you into a corner and make you feel as if you're all alone. He wants you to believe there's no hope and you can't press forward from where you are!

The enemy will try to have you all up in your feelings: depressed, stressed out, fearful, worried, feeling like you need to kill yourself. The devil knows that when you're in your feelings, you're not in faith. When you're not in faith, he can come against you. This is when God sends someone your way for Him to use to snatch you out of that horrible pit and restore you again. They pray you through, to restore you to good health, having the right mindset and the right focus. They pray you through to getting your power back, walking in victory, speaking with authority, and knowing who you are in Christ Jesus.

Although the enemy tries to separate you from everyone, and us from each other, God is the God who never fails. He is the only true living God, our Lord and Savior Jesus Christ, and He'll always send a willing vessel to bring us back together again.

When unified, we can remain strong in faith with God and His Word. We must have each other around to encourage us when tough times come. In difficult circumstances, we inspire each other to keep living, keep striving, to never give up or give in. We must pray each other through!

The enemy is trying to cause division during this Covid-19 pandemic with battles over who is vaccinated and who is not; who's wearing a mask and who's not; and who's voting for this person and who's not.

Remember, Family, the devil is a whole lie!

Division is also linked to unforgiveness. You may become stuck where you are, missing out on what God has for you. You may miss out on how God wants to use you all because you don't want to forgive those that hurt you, misused you, or did you wrong. We have to forgive!

We'll get into how unforgiveness can contaminate your faith in Part 6. For now, know that we have to forgive to be unified. We as the body of Christ need to learn how to stick together no matter what.

We must love each other no matter what.

Pray for each other no matter what.

Support each other no matter what.

Look out for each other no matter what.

Look at the unity in the Upper Room on the day of Pentecost. God's Word says the disciples were all in one accord, waiting for the fulfilled promise of the Holy Spirit. And the Holy Spirit showed up!

Matthew 18:15-17 NLT

"If another believer sins against you, go privately and point out the offense. If the other person listens and confesses it, you have won that person back. But if you are unsuccessful, take one or two others with you and go back again, so that everything you say may be confirmed by two or three witnesses. If the person still refuses to listen, take your case to the church. Then if he or she won't accept the church's decision, treat that person as a pagan or a corrupt tax collector."

Jesus is teaching us about how devastating it can be when you let a person of division go unchecked. God created and established us, the Church, to be the problem solvers not the creators of division.

You can't allow your faith to be contaminated by fear, worrying, pressure, negative thoughts, wrongful speaking, bitterness, and division.

We need to serve notice to the enemy that, not only are we sticking with Jesus, we're sticking together! Nobody gets left behind, not on our watch. Nobody loses, because nobody accepts defeat. We're coming out of every tough time and circumstance better, stronger, wiser. We are ready to do everything God anointed us to do and claim everything God has in store for us.

Ephesians 4:3-7 NLT

"Make every effort to keep yourselves united in the Spirit, binding yourselves together with peace. For there is one body and one Spirit, just as you have been called to one glorious hope for the future. There is one Lord, one faith, one baptism, one God and Father of all, who is over all, in all, and living through all. However, he has given each one of us a special gift through the generosity of Christ."

When you go to hear an orchestra, many times the first notes you hear are chaotic as each individual player warms up on their instrument. The violin player plays her own tune. The oboe player plays his own tune. The result is cacophony. But when the conductor walks onto the stage, all of the players submit to his direction, and beautiful music is the result.

In other words, there is strength in unity. There is power in unity, and unity glorifies God like nothing else. The book of John contains the longest prayer by Jesus recorded in the Bible (John Chapter 17). The main concern of that prayer is unity among God's people, which signifies the power and importance of unity. Jesus prayed for all believers, in all times, to become unified. When the body of Christ comes together with one common purpose, we can change the world.

We must work together across racial, cultural, and socioeconomic boundaries to spread the love and hope of Jesus Christ to a dying world. Since unity is so important to Jesus, it should be just as important to us. Take a few moments right now to pray for unity in these areas: your personal life, your family, your church, your job, and your community.

Family, don't let your faith become contaminated by division, but remain strong in faith by sticking together with God's Word as your foundation!

#ByFaithWeGood

PART 6

UNFORGIVENESS

Romans 1:16-17 KJV

"For I am not ashamed of the gospel of Christ: for it is the power of God unto salvation to every one that believeth; to the Jew first, and also to the Greek. For therein is the righteousness of God revealed from faith to faith: as it is written, The just shall live by faith."

We go from faith to faith. God takes us from faith to faith.

We're created to live from faith to faith. From the beginning to the end, from start to finish. Family, we have to go from faith to faith!

We cannot be ashamed of loving God, serving God, trusting God, and committing our lives to being in and maintaining a personal relationship with Him.

You have to function by faith in the Kingdom of God. The power of faith is to turn your situation to your advantage. This cannot take place if you're not acting in faith. There are things that can contaminate our faith, and make us ineffective for God, ourselves, and others. There are ways about us that we allow at times to contaminate our faith and negatively affect what we believe.

I know, Family, you've read this already, but we have to make sure we receive this understanding and Godly wisdom. We have to apply it to our lives by faith, staying focused and always remaining strong in faith. We must never waver or doubt. We must not allow ourselves to get caught up in our feelings but instead be rooted and grounded in God's Word. Yes, living this way is possible!

The next subject we're going to focus on that can contaminate your faith is **Unforgiveness**.

UNFORGIVENESS

Definition: When you're unwilling or unable to forgive; when you are unwill-

Unforgiveness is an area in life with which many struggle at times. This is often because of situations that caused severe emotional pain, like betrayal from someone you felt was the only one you could depend on. We're all guilty of offending other people, and we've all been offended by other people; that's the fact of living in a sinful world. But we learn through God's Word that forgiveness is part of God's love being reflected in the midst of tough times. We must forgive even when someone close to you has done something that causes you to separate yourself from them and want absolutely nothing to do with them.

It's impossible to live a victorious Christian life with unforgiveness in our hearts. Unforgiveness is not of God. If you allow something that is not of God to take root in your life, then you're allowing your faith to be contaminated. You're positioning yourself to be ineffective in the way God called and created you to live and what He's called you to do. Flowing with unforgiveness affects what you believe and puts you out of alignment with God and His Word.

It isn't the offense that destroys relationships. It's the inability to forgive.

Unforgiveness is poison to the soul. Unforgiveness is a sin that locks the unforgiving person in their own self-made prison. It's as bad as being enslaved to mind-altering drugs or alcoholism. Unforgiveness is a sin that will destroy its own container. Unforgiveness is a sin that will destroy you like an incurable cancer. Unforgiveness is a sin that causes bitterness in your life.

Flowing in unforgiveness causes you to be in your feelings. This is why I share with you all the time that faith and your feelings cannot coexist. If you're in your feelings, you're not in faith. And if you're not in faith, you are not covered. It's faith that activates God's Word and what God promised to bring to life in our lives. It's one thing to be covered because of God's grace and His favor. God will cover you just because of the love He has for you. But there will be times in your life when you'll need to be in faith, being "strong in the Lord, and in the power of his might" (Ephesians 6:10 KJV).

Jesus said in Mark 11:25-26, "And whenever you stand praying, if you have anything against anyone, forgive him, that your Father in heaven may also forgive you your trespasses. But if you do not forgive, neither will your Father in heaven forgive your trespasses" (NKJV).

This isn't about our eternal salvation. That is secure when we put our faith in Jesus Christ as our Lord and Savior. This is about our being blessed or disciplined by God (Hebrews 12:7-11). God will not hear our prayers when we have unforgiveness in our hearts (Isaiah 59:1-2).

People often say, "I don't get mad, I get even." People mistakenly believe that their bitterness and refusal to forgive will make the other person suffer.

But it's the unforgiving person that suffers!

How can we be effective in fulfilling our God-given purpose if we're flowing with things that are not like God and or against His will? How can we move mountains? How can we pull down strongholds? How can we be effective with the power God has given us to tread upon serpents and scorpions and over all the power of the enemy (Luke 10:19)?

Nothing shall by any means hurt you when you don't allow your faith to be contaminated simply because you don't want to forgive. This is not even including other situations that you may allow to take root that will contaminate your faith. As with those, you must watch out for unforgiveness.

Colossians 3:13-14 NLT
"Make allowance for each other's faults, and forgive anyone who offends you. Remember, the Lord forgave you, so you must forgive others. Above all, clothe yourselves with love, which binds us all together in perfect harmony."

Two of the main responsibilities we have in order to be in alignment with God and His Word—in order to be like Jesus—is to love and forgive. At times, these seem like the hardest things to do for many in the body of Christ. Once again, God will not hear our prayers when we have unforgiveness in our hearts. When you don't want to forgive someone, you're basically being proud, as if you have a right to not forgive. You've made up your mind: "I said what I said, and I ain't doing it." Somehow you still think that everything moving forward is going to be peaches and cream. You think that even if you don't properly align yourself with God, you will still be able to move forward in a better way.

You think, "Man, I'm not forgiving them, but I'm still gonna get my blessing."

"I'm not forgiving them, but I'm still gonna get promoted."

"I'm not forgiving them, but I'm still believing in God for increase."

God's Word says in James 4:5-6:

"Do ye think that the scripture saith in vain, The spirit that dwelleth in us lusteth to envy? But he giveth more grace. Wherefore he saith, God resisteth the proud, but giveth grace unto the humble." (KJV)

"Do you think the Scriptures have no meaning? They say that God is passionate that the spirit he has placed within us should be faithful to him. And he gives grace generously. As the Scriptures say, 'God opposes the proud but gives grace to the humble.'" (NLT)

You can't think you don't have to do what God said, and you're still gonna be all that and a bag of chips! Not only will your faith be contaminated, but you'll find yourself bound by flowing in unforgiveness. You have to be humble, and take heed to God's Word to do the right thing.

Romans 12:17-19 New King James Version
"Repay no one evil for evil. Have regard for good things in the sight of all men. If it is possible, as much as depends on you, live peaceably with all men. Beloved, do not avenge yourselves, but rather give place to wrath; for it is written, 'Vengeance is Mine, I will repay,' says the Lord."

Unforgiveness doesn't yield the right of vengeance to the Lord; the bitter person wants to become his own god and becomes his own worst enemy, destroying himself. Unforgiveness and bitterness are often hidden sins. No one may notice your bitterness and unforgiveness at first, but the poison is doing its hidden work inside your heart.

Unforgiveness is often a family sin. Husbands won't forgive their wives. Wives won't forgive their husbands. Children won't forgive their parents, and parents won't forgive their children.

Unforgiveness among fellow believers is common. I know Christians who will not talk to each other, cannot even look at each other, and wouldn't dare sit on the same side of the sanctuary. There are pastors who will not forgive church members, and believers who will not forgive their pastor. It's easy to see why there are so many prayerless and powerless churches!

Ephesians 4:31-32 NKJV

"Let all bitterness, wrath, anger, clamor, and evil speaking be put away from you, with all malice. And be kind to one another, tenderhearted, forgiving one another, even as God in Christ forgave you."

Colossians 3:13-14 NKJV

"Bearing with one another, and forgiving one another, if anyone has a complaint against another; even as Christ forgave you, so you also must do. But above all these things put on love, which is the bond of perfection."

The forgiveness of people for their sins toward us will never make a wrong right. The hurt, pain, and memory are still there. However, even if someone doesn't apologize, we must release them so we won't bring ourselves into the bondage of unforgiveness. Being bound in the prison of unforgiveness is a sad way to live our lives. Even if the abuser repents, sometimes the abused still holds on to the hurt that's been done to them. This only puts themselves in the prison of unforgiveness. Only the power of the Holy Spirit can give us the grace to truly forgive.

Someone once said, "Forgiveness is agreeing to live with the consequences of another person's sin." Forgiveness is costly; we pay the price of the evil we forgive. You're going to live with those consequences whether you want to or not; your only choice is whether you will live in the bitterness of unforgiveness or the freedom of forgiveness. When Jesus forgave you, He took the consequences of your sin upon Himself. All true forgiveness is substitutional; no one really forgives without bearing the penalty of the other person's sin. Forgiveness is extending mercy to those who have harmed us.

It's the spiritually strong and brave person who knows how to forgive. We're to make a constant effort to forgive so that we can build a forgiving mindset in our brain. Matthew 18:21-23 says that Peter said to Jesus, "'Lord, how often shall my brother sin against me, and I forgive him? Up to seven times?' Jesus said to him, "I do not say to you, up to seven times, but up to seventy times seven'" (NKJV). Living a lifestyle of forgiveness is commanded for Christians: Forgive as the Lord forgave you (Colossians 3:13).

It's mandatory to forgive, even if you have to separate yourself from other people, like when the ones you thought were for you are exposed. As we've heard people say, their true colors come out! When someone does or says something wrong to you, you don't have to be around them, but you do have to forgive them. As God continues to work on you, you'll get better at walking in love. When you see them again, there'll be no negative vibes or intentions. Instead you'll give God all the glory because of how much you've grown.

Forgiveness is for you too, not just the other person. Nine times out of ten, they're moving forward and living their life while you're held back. You're stuck waiting for everything you're believing God for and wondering, "Why ain't this happening?" You're caught up in your feelings as your faith is being contaminated. You're flowing in a way that is blocking what God wants to do through you and for you.

To forgive is to be set free, not to be weighted down, held back, or stagnant.

To forgive is to move forward.

To forgive is to release yourself from your past.

To forgive is to move by faith and not according to your feelings.

What God has in store for you will be greater than anything anybody has ever done or said to you. Family, God will always give you the strength you need to do what is right and not allow pride to get in the way. You never have to feel as though when you forgive, the other person is getting away with something. Because you love the Lord and you take ownership of being called according to His purpose, all things are always working for your good (Romans 8:28).

Family, stay focused and always press forward by faith!

#ByFaithWeGood

WHAT ARE YOU SUSTAINING THAT'S CONTAMINATING YOUR FAITH?

Pride, Ego, Drama, Hatred, Jealousy, Envy, Slander, Strife, Malice

Romans 1:16-17 KJV

"For I am not ashamed of the gospel of Christ: for it is the power of God unto salvation to every one that believeth; to the Jew first, and also to the Greek. For therein is the righteousness of God revealed from faith to faith: as it is written, The just shall live by faith."

We go from faith to faith. God takes us from faith to faith. We're created to live from faith to Faith. From the beginning to the end, from start to finish. We cannot be ashamed to love God, to serve God, to trust God, to commit our life to being in, and maintaining a personal relationship with Him!

You have to function by faith in the Kingdom of God. The power of faith is to turn your situation to your advantage. This cannot take place if you're not acting in faith. There are things that can contaminate our faith, and make us ineffective for God, ourselves, and others. There are ways about us that we allow at times to contaminate our faith and negatively affect what we believe.

I'm telling you, Family, the more you read this, the more you're establishing God's Word within you. By the time you finish reading this book, you're going to be walking in the power of faith: turning every situation to your advantage!

Before you get there, Family, there is more work to be done.

What are you sustaining?
What are you sustaining that's contaminating your faith? Is it pride or your ego? Is it your comfortability, because you are afraid to step outside of your comfort zone?

There are things that you will sustain in your life at times that will contaminate your faith. You sustain these things because you like to play it safe. Some of the things that you can sustain are your pride, your ego, and self-centeredness. As humans, we always want to be comfortable. We love to be comfortable. We love not having to do certain things or go to certain places or approach certain people. So we don't. I know this to be true for myself. Most of us hate discomfort, but I have learned in my own life that I perform best when I am uncomfortable.

What are you sustaining just so you can stay comfortable? In these Parts 7 and 8, we will look at some things that you may be sustaining, starting with pride.

PRIDE

Pride can contaminate your faith, because it's often driven by poor self-worth and shame. You may feel so badly about yourself that you compensate by feeling superior. You look for others' flaws as a way to conceal your own. You relish criticizing others as a defense against recognizing your own shortcomings.

Pride prevents us from acknowledging our human vulnerabilities. This shame-driven pride makes us too uncomfortable to say, "I'm sorry. I was wrong. I made a mistake." When pride rules, we believe we're always right. This makes it difficult to sustain intimate relationships; nobody likes being with a know-it-all.

As the light of our dignity shines more brightly, we realize that we don't have to be perfect. Showing vulnerability and humility invites people toward us. We become approachable rather than intimidating. We don't see ourselves as better or worse than anyone else. We recognize that we're all part of the human condition; we all have strengths and weaknesses. Pride can contaminate your faith, because it causes you to not forgive. Pride will make you insecure, not wanting to look a certain way to other people. Instead of doing the right thing and making things right, you hold back and don't care.

It is freeing to walk in the dignity that comes from simply being human. We don't need to achieve "greatness" to have worth and value.

We're great just as we are. We might be inclined to pursue excellence because it feels meaningful, enlivening, and expansive, but we must not let it define who we are as a person. When pride replaces our human dignity, it disconnects us from God and others. By affirming our dignity and allowing others their dignity, we become more available to honor ourselves and connect with others as equals. Pride is a burden we don't need. Living with dignity, by faith according to God's Word, allows us to move more freely through life.

Proverbs 11:2 NIV
"When pride comes, then comes disgrace, but with humility comes wisdom."

Pride distorts decision-making abilities. An arrogant, conceited, or haughty person will make costly mistakes, but a humble and modest man will clearly see right and wrong, truth and error, wisdom and folly. Your greatness depends on getting rid of all pride.

God inspired King Solomon to be your personal counselor through the book of Proverbs. The wisest king that ever lived wrote down important advice for your success and prosperity. Pride will cause you to make foolish choices that will shame you; humility will lead you to make wise choices. The worst thing you can have is pride. It will cost you more than any other character fault. Conceit will deceive you into folly, which will quickly and surely shame you. Humility, on the other hand, leads to wisdom, which protects men from foolish mistakes and disgrace.

Do you grasp the importance of this lesson? You will never hear or read a more important warning for your life. Pride will destroy you, and it will destroy you disgracefully and shamefully before all men. Humility will lift you up before both God and good men.

EGO

While the ego can yield positive results, an unhealthy ego can thrust all of that positivity into reverse. One study found that over-exerting your ego can lead to exhaustion, therefore depleting your willpower to stick to healthy habits.

Your ego can also cause you to not step up and do the right things. Pride and your ego can cause you to be unforgiving. Your ego can position you against making a wrong right. Your ego wants to keep a wrong wrong, while making you think you have a right.

Remember the devil is a whole lie!

DRAMA

Drama means to create an uncomfortable feeling through manipulation and/or control.

Even simpler? Drama means made-up conflict.

Drama will contaminate your faith.

HATRED

Hatred can be described as an intense dislike. You can never properly align yourself with God with hatred in your heart.

How can we be effective in fulfilling our God-given purpose if we're flowing with things that are not like God or against His will? How can we move mountains? How can we pull down strongholds? How can we be effective with the power God has given us to to tread upon serpents and scorpions and over all the power of the enemy? With nothing shall by any means hurting us when and if your faith is contaminated? Simply because you don't want to let go of being prideful? This is not even including other situations that you may allow to take root that will contaminate your faith.

That's why God's Word says in James 4:5-6:

"Do ye think that the scripture saith in vain, The spirit that dwelleth in us lusteth to envy? But he giveth more grace. Wherefore he saith, God resisteth the proud, but giveth grace unto the humble." (KJV)

"Do you think the Scriptures have no meaning? They say that God is passionate that the spirit he has placed within us should be faithful to him. And he gives grace generously. As the Scriptures say, 'God opposes the proud but gives grace to the humble.'" (NLT)

You can't think you don't have to do what God said, and you're still gonna be all that and a bag of chips! Not only will your faith be contaminated, but you'll find yourself bound. You have to be humble, and take heed to God's Word to do the right thing. Family, make up your mind and have a desire for God to transform you! Transformation and remaining strong in faith comes when you renew your mind.

The fallen world and sinful man are all too ready to squeeze us into their own mold and cultivate in us a worldly mindset where God is far removed. Our own sin nature rebels against the Spirit of God who dwells within us. We lust after our own fleshly desires, but God uses Paul to warn us in Romans 12:2 to "be not conformed to this world: but be ye transformed by the renewing of your mind" (KJV).

This is a daily transformation process as we are changed from glory to glory, into the image and likeness of Christ as we abide in Him and He in us. It is a lifelong process that requires vigilance at all times. The enemy of our soul desires to shipwreck our faith and render our testimony impotent, either by stroking our ego or by causing us to become fearful. The enemy is a deceiver and a murderer and has been from the beginning. We need to put on the armor of God, day by day, if we are to overcome the world, our flesh, and the devil.

We have an opportunity to allow God into the deepest parts of our heart and mind, for Him to do a transformational work within us. In our own efforts, we may be unable to see a way out of bad habits or bad thinking. We must allow God's Holy Spirit to renew our minds, to renew our strength, to renew our focus, and to renew our lives in their entirety.

JEALOUSY

Jealousy will have you blocking your own blessing because you're too busy being mad about somebody else's blessing!

Like pride, jealousy may be driven by low self-esteem or a poor self-image. If you don't feel valuable and confident, it can be hard to truly believe that you are who God said you are. Being jealous will make it hard to truly believe in your worth. Jealousy makes it hard for you to believe you're worth everything God has in store for you. You may end up blocking your own blessing because you're too busy being mad about what's happening in someone else's life instead of positioning yourself for what God wants to do in your life.

Family, ask yourself, what are you sustaining that's contaminating your faith?

When you sustain one thing, it can give birth to something else. Watch this, Family, because jealousy can cause envy.

ENVY

Jealousy and envy are connected. Being envious is also a feeling of discontent or resentful longing aroused by someone else's possessions, qualities, and blessings.

Being envious is the desire to have a quality, possession, or attractive attribute belonging to someone else. When you allow envy to take root in your life, it contaminates your faith. God can't use you because you're too busy envying and pushing away the people God wants to draw closer to Himself through you.

Family. What are you sustaining that's getting in the way of God's will and Word being fulfilled in your life, contaminating your faith?

Come on, let's connect the dots. Jealousy leads to envy. Guess what envy leads to?

SLANDER

Slander is the action or crime of making a false spoken statement damaging to a person's reputation.

You're jealous and envious. Now you want to spread rumors. Suddenly you find yourself making false and damaging statements about someone.

Family, hear me, and hear me clearly: You cannot function like this as part of the Kingdom of God!

Not only that, but being jealous, envious, and slanderous will also give birth to strife.

STRIFE

Strife is being angry or bitter and being in disagreement to the point of conflict. You can't come into agreement with anybody, nor can you align yourself with what God said in Matthew 18:19-20: "Again I say unto you, That if two of you shall agree on earth as touching anything that they shall ask, it shall be done for them of my Father which is in heaven. For where two or three are gathered together in my name, there am I in the midst of them" (KJV).

Like we learned in part 5 of this series, there is power in unity. However, once strife comes into play, malice is quickly birthed. All of these are connected!

MALICE

Once malice comes into play, you're at the point where you don't even care that all these others are present. Malice is the intention or desire to do evil; it is an ill will. At this point you have no conscience; you literally do not care. You become reckless and will go above and beyond to get ahead, damage, scheme against, or hurt someone.

Family. What are you sustaining that's contaminating your faith?

For a lot of you, getting rid of these things starts with forgiveness. These things took root in your life because of something that happened or something that someone did to you growing up. This is where you need God to step in, so you can let it go. Only He can help you move forward with your life into all that He has for you and how He wants to use you.

Family, you're created by God to love and live an empowered life and to help others do the same. Stay focused, let Jesus lead you, and always press forward by faith.

#ByFaithWeGood

PART 9

ANXIETY, DEPRESSION, FRUSTRATION

Romans 1:16-17 KJV
"For I am not ashamed of the gospel of Christ: for it is the power of
God unto salvation to every one that believeth; to the Jew first, and
also to the Greek. For therein is the righteousness of God revealed
from faith to faith: as it is written, The just shall live by faith."

We go from faith to faith. God takes us from faith to faith. We're created to live from faith to faith. From the beginning to the end, from start to finish. We cannot be ashamed of loving God, serving God, trusting God, and committing our lives to being in and maintaining a personal relationship with Him.

Some well-known areas of life that can contaminate your faith are **Anxiety, Depression,** and **Frustration**. How does having these emotions at play in your life contaminate your faith?

ANXIETY

Anxiety is a feeling of fear, dread, and uneasiness. It might cause you to sweat, feel restless and tense, and have a rapid heartbeat. It can be a normal reaction to stress.

For example, you might feel anxious when faced with a difficult problem at work, before taking a test, or before making an important decision. Anxiety can also cause:

• stomach pain, nausea, or digestive trouble
• headaches
• insomnia or other sleep issues (waking up frequently, for example)
• weakness or fatigue
• rapid breathing or shortness of breath

• pounding heart or increased heart rate
• sweating
• trembling or shaking
• muscle tension or pain

Anxiety can also lead to panic attacks, as anxiety can be a bodily response to stress.[1]

DEPRESSION

According to Psychiatry.org, "depression (major depressive disorder) is a common and serious medical illness that negatively affects how you feel, the way you think, and how you act."[2] "Depression is a mental condition characterized by feelings of severe despondency and dejection, typically also with feelings of inadequacy and guilt, often accompanied by lack of energy and disturbance of appetite and sleep."[3]

"Depression causes feelings of sadness and or a loss of interest in activities you once enjoyed. It can lead to a variety of emotional and physical problems and can decrease your ability to function at work and at home.

"Depression symptoms can vary from mild to severe and can include:

• feeling sad or having a depressed mood
• loss of interest or pleasure in activities once enjoyed
• changes in appetite — weight loss or gain unrelated to dieting
• trouble sleeping or sleeping too much
• loss of energy or increased fatigue
• increase in purposeless physical activity (e.g., inability to sit still,

[1] Kimberly Holland, "Everything You Need to Know About Anxiety," Healthline, Sept. 3, 2020, https://www.healthline.com/health/anxiety.

[2] Felix Torres, M.D., MBA, DFAPA, "What is Depression?" American Psychiatric Association, October 2020, https://psychiatry.org/patients-families/depression/what-is-depression.

[3] "Depression," River Park Psychology Consultants LLC, 2022, https://www.riverpark-psych.com/depression.

pacing, handwringing) or slowed movements or speech (these actions must be severe enough to be observable by others)
• feeling worthless or guilty
• difficulty thinking, concentrating or making decisions
• thoughts of death or suicide"[4]

FRUSTRATION

Frustration is the feeling of being upset or annoyed, especially because of inability to change or achieve something. You can be frustrated by people, places and things. You can be frustrated by the prevention of the progress, success, or fulfillment of something. Not only can these frustrate you, but frustration can also block you from succeeding and achieving something.

Frustration can give birth to anger and hatred. It can destroy relationships. It can stem from a lack of patience or prayer. Frustration can come about because we aren't dwelling in God's Word or we're lacking trust in God that is developed through getting to know Him and having a personal relationship with Him.

Frustration can also be a deep chronic sense or state of insecurity and dissatisfaction arising from unresolved problems or unfulfilled needs. For some people, when problems come, they sweep them under the rug, always trying to avoid actually dealing with the problems. Frustration comes in because they never dealt with the problem. The same problems keep appearing throughout their lives, never going away.

Instead of sustaining the problem, you need the Holy Spirit to help you solve the problem so that it goes away. When you are frustrated due to unfulfilled needs, it is often pride or insecurities that hold you back. Because of pride, you don't communicate and let others know what you need. Insecurities can set in. You become frustrated because you don't have what you need when all you have to do is open your mouth and say something.

---

[4] *Torres, "What is Depression?"*

Know this about Anxiety, Depression, and Frustration, Family: God did not create you to function like this in the earth. God created you to have a relationship with Him, to trust Him, to fully depend on Him at all times in all circumstances. The enemy will use these three areas to contaminate your faith, to throw you off balance, and to cause dysfunction in your marriage, in your family, and even on your job. You have to "be strong in the Lord, and in the power of his might" (Ephesians 6:10 KJV). You have to have God's Word as your foundation. In order to renew your mind, you have to go to God first. In order to be strong in faith, you have to be grounded in God's Word. By faith, God's Word will come alive in your life and become your reality.

Family, in order to keep your faith from being contaminated, you have to have scriptures in your mind. God's Word teaches you to deal with specific areas in your life that need to be dealt with and dealt with God's way. In order to maintain your faith, you have to use God's Word. God has a word—literally a scripture—for any and every thing you will ever go through in life. If you find Anxiety, Depression, and Frustration contaminating your faith, remember what the Word of the Lord says in Philippians 4:8-9:

"Finally, brethren, whatsoever things are true, whatsoever things are honest, whatsoever things are just, whatsoever things are pure, whatsoever things are lovely, whatsoever things are of good report; if there be any virtue, and if there be any praise, think on these things. Those things, which ye have both learned, and received, and heard, and seen in me, do: and the God of peace shall be with you." (KJV)

We are to feed our minds with blessings from God and the good things we can find in our lives or situations. We are to think about what is true rather than the lies Satan would try and have us believe. We are to dwell on what is noble and right so our actions will follow our thoughts.

Paul seems to indicate he could have written a length about rejoicing in the Lord (Philippians 4:4) and God's peace. These were certainly topics he would have enjoyed. Instead, he summarizes a list of areas of importance for believers. They include what is true, lovely, just, commendable, pure, excellent, honorable, and praiseworthy.

As believers, we "think on these things" while God guards our hearts (Philippians 4:7). We are also commanded to focus our lives on things that please God. As children of God, we have been brought into a relationship with God through our union with Jesus Christ by faith. We are expected to take responsibility for walking in spirit and truth; living as unto the Lord; trusting in the Word of God; depending on our Heavenly Father; submitting to the Holy Spirit; abiding in Christ; and appropriating all that is ours in Christ by faith.

Philippians 4:9 even says, "Those things, which ye have both learned, and received, and heard, and seen in me, do: and the God of peace shall be with you" (KJV). Just hearing and reading the Word of God is not enough, especially when it comes to Anxiety, Depression, and Frustration contaminating your faith. Actually obeying and applying to our lives what we learn through God's Word is what brings peace and wisdom. The battle for right choices begins in our minds. Our Creator gave us an incredible brain with the ability to do great things in life, including thinking. Many times our thoughts lead us in a downward spiral and our attitudes quickly follow. We have the power of Christ enabling us to stop those negative defeating thoughts. Go back and look at Philippians 4:7 where the Word of the Lord says, "And the peace of God, which passeth all understanding, shall keep your hearts and minds through Christ Jesus" (KJV).

When we pray and seek God, spend time meditating on His word, and trust Him in all situations, we experience God's peace. No one can give peace like the Lord. He alone is our refuge who protects, comforts, and strengthens us at all times. It's such a blessing and encouragement to know that God is always in control. Know that God is not disappointed, upset, frustrated, or angry with you. He's at peace with you. Let that peacefulness you have with and from God change how you approach Him today and everyday. God is our strength! His peace is with us all every day of our lives.

God's peace passes all understanding and keeps our hearts and minds through Christ Jesus (Philippians 4:7). Even in your most difficult times, God's peace is with you. When we focus on the things of God, the peace of God will follow. With a proper focus on positive things, we can experience peace through the power of God.

Ephesians 3:19 KJV
"And to know the love of Christ, which passeth knowledge, that ye
might be filled with all the fulness of God."

Paul wants his readers to experience the love of Christ in a way that
goes beyond mere understanding. This does not imply that knowledge
is unimportant. Instead, Paul wants the Ephesians to understand that
God's love is ultimately beyond comprehension. Family, so that your
faith won't be contaminated, have a desire to be filled with the Spirit of
God. This way, Anxiety, Depression, and Frustration can't take root in
your life. God in many ways is and always will be the only One who
can keep, sustain, and truly satisfy us. He is the only One who will
never disappoint us.

Ephesians 3:20-21 KJV
"Now unto him that is able to do exceeding abundantly above all that
we ask or think, according to the power that worketh in us, unto him
be glory in the church by Christ Jesus throughout all ages, world without end. Amen."

You might be in a season of pruning right now, where everything feels
out of whack. You might be in a drought season, where you feel
parched and tired and ready to give up. You might be in a season of
questioning how to receive. No matter where you're at today, know
this: God will never leave you. He's with you every step of the way,
even if others aren't. God is with you in all seasons.

Family, I don't know where you find yourself today, but this I do know:
Through strong faith, God will do exceedingly abundantly beyond all
that you can ask or think! God loves you more than you can fathom.
We can trust in God. We might not always like the process, but we can
trust the designer of the process. God always wants the best for you.
Above all, He wants your heart to be fully for Him.

We serve God, the only true Living God, our Lord and Savior Jesus
Christ, who specializes in doing the impossible. He can do beyond
what we can ask, ever imagine, or think of! God knows best, and He
will never let you fail. Let the Lord lead you. "Unto him be glory in the
church by Christ Jesus throughout all ages, world without end" (Ephesians 3:21 KJV), in Jesus' Name, Amen!

56

You don't have to be frustrated if you trust God. Get to know Him. Have a personal relationship with Him. When you know God, you'll always trust Him. May the grace of the Lord Jesus Christ, the love of God, and the fellowship of the Holy Spirit be with you all. With God, you'll never fail, you'll never lose, and you'll never be defeated—you will always win.

#ByFaithWeGood

PART 10

LACK OF PRAYER, LACK OF PRAISE & WORSHIP TO GOD, LACK OF FAITHFULNESS, & DISOBEDIENCE

Romans 1:16-17 KJV

"For I am not ashamed of the gospel of Christ: for it is the power of God unto salvation to every one that believeth; to the Jew first, and also to the Greek. For therein is the righteousness of God revealed from faith to faith: as it is written, The just shall live by faith."

We go from faith to faith. God takes us from faith to faith. We're created to live from faith to faith. From the beginning to the end, from start to finish. We cannot be ashamed of loving God, serving God, trusting God, and committing our lives to being in and maintaining a personal relationship with Him!

You have to function by faith in the Kingdom of God. The power of faith is to turn your situation to your advantage. This cannot take place if you're not acting in faith. There are things that can contaminate our faith, and make us ineffective for God, ourselves, and others. There are ways about us that we allow at times to contaminate our faith and negatively affect what we believe.

Family, to live a life of faith, our foundation is in having a personal relationship with Jesus Christ and standing on God's Word alone. In order for our faith to be sustained and not contaminated, there are also areas in which we cannot lack.

We cannot effectively live the life God created us to live and fulfill the purpose God created us to fulfill if we are flowing with lack of prayer, lack of praise and worship to God, lack of faithfulness, and disobedience.

When you lack in these areas, your faith is not being sustained. You're not in alignment with God and His Word.

LACK OF PRAYER

You can not be victorious if you don't have a prayer life. Having a prayer life, and spending time in God's Word is absolutely necessary.

If I can use an analogy, the longer a tea bag sits in a cup of water, the stronger the tea. In the same way, the more God's Word saturates our minds, the more we seek God. The more we seek His will instead of our own personal desires, the clearer our grasp will be on what's important to God and the stronger our prayers will be!

We are to pray without ceasing. Prayer connects us to the power of God, which is necessary to defeat spiritual enemies. Prayer must become a daily, constant, and consistent way of living. In any given moment, we are only a thought and breath away from communicating with God. Prayer is to permeate believers' lives at all times. Praying in the spirit is a form of worship, enabled by the Holy Spirit who intercedes on our behalf. When we pray, we are praying not just for ourselves but for all saints, all of God's children. You can sustain your faith by declaring the Word of the Lord through prayer because "faith comes by hearing, and hearing by the Word of God" (Romans 10:17 NKJV). Your faith is being fed when you declare and hear the Word of God.

Your prayer life cannot afford to lack, Family. You're not in communication with God if you're not praying. Lacking in prayer, you can be completely unaware of your spiritual surroundings and become easily distracted. If you're not praying, you're leaving yourself and your family hanging, because you're not maintaining the responsibility of covering yourselves in prayer. Being uncovered gives the enemy an opportunity to come against you and your family. We fight the enemy and claim our rights as children of God through prayer.

The Lord is ready and available to help all who call on Him. He is ready to hear and answer the prayers of His people. There's power in our prayers. When you feel like there's nothing you can do, remember God can!

Prayer is communicating with God for direction. It is casting all your cares on Him because He cares for you (2 Peter 5:7). Prayer empowers you. Prayer keeps your feet in a firm position. You are believing God for what He wants to do in your life, as well as taking ownership of who God created you to be.

Prayer through faith is a weapon that will destroy your opposition openly. There's power in praying in the Name of Jesus. No matter what the enemy may try, he can't touch our relationship with God. Prayer will destroy the enemy and anything he tries. At the same time, prayer will encourage your heart. Prayer will increase your joy and faith, knowing God will always show up for you.

LACK OF PRAISE & WORSHIP TO GOD

Giving God praise, worshiping Him in spirit and in truth, must be a priority in our lives.

Psalm 150:1-6 KJV
"Praise ye the LORD. Praise God in his sanctuary: praise him in the firmament of his power. Praise him for his mighty acts: praise him according to his excellent greatness. Praise him with the sound of the trumpet: praise him with the psaltery and harp. Praise him with the timbrel and dance: praise him with stringed instruments and organs. Praise him upon the loud cymbals: praise him upon the high sounding cymbals. Let everything that hath breath praise the LORD. Praise ye the LORD."

John 4:23-24 KJV
"But the hour cometh, and now is, when the true worshippers shall worship the Father in spirit and in truth: for the Father seeketh such to worship him. God is a Spirit: and they that worship him must worship him in spirit and in truth."

Praise is something we should do everyday, all day. Praise ought to be a part of our everyday lives. Regardless as to what is going on in our lives, we should not let anything or anybody separate us from the love or steal the joy we have in Jesus. We serve a mighty God! Because of who He is, we should give Him a mighty praise!

Worship is an act of offering. When we give ourselves over to God in worship, we reveal our love for Him. Offering your praise, love, and life to God is an essential aspect of being His child.

Worship is not just an act that happens in church on Sunday mornings. It is a lifestyle that drives us to desire becoming more like Jesus. Notice that God is seeking true worshipers. God has not lost any of His children and he is searching for those among His children who are worshiping Him in spirit and in truth.

The question then becomes, "Why is He seeking true worshipers?" God is a God of love. He loves His children so much that He wants to shower them with all they need for an abundant life here on earth. God wants to bless and give his children favor beyond measure, but He cannot do so if we as His children do not worship Him in the manner that He wants to be worshiped.

Praise: to commend, to applaud or magnify.

Praise to God is an expression of worshiping, lifting up, and glorifying the Lord.

Worship: to ascribe worth, to pay homage, to reverence.

We have been called to lift up the name of Jesus, humble ourselves, and adore Him. The problem is that many people worship with other concerns on their minds that distract them from genuine worship.

It is not enough to just show up to worship and sit through a service. Jesus wants more than that: He wants genuine worship from your heart. We are to applaud or lift up the name of Jesus in His sanctuary and everywhere we go. This means worshiping beyond church. It means that any and every time that we are in the presence of God, we have reason to offer Him praise. When He wakes us up in the morning, we have a reason to offer Him praise. When He puts food on our table, we have reason to offer Him praise. When God gets us to and from places safely, we have a reason to give God praise! Every place that we are in is a sanctuary because we are never out of the presence of God.

Worship enables us to maintain our faith, keeping it from being contaminated. We sustain our faith by living in a way, maintaining a lifestyle that is pleasing to God. You have to have faith to even give God praise, to worship Him and to call on Him. The Bible says that "without faith it is impossible to please God" (Hebrews 11:6 NIV). In other words, without faith you can't get God's attention.

Giving God praise will keep your faith from being contaminated, because your praise and worship is a weapon. Praise and worship will position you to bounce back in tough times. Praise and worship to God will increase and strengthen your faith. You will believe God can renew your strength so you can break out of how you feel, call on the name of the Lord, and get what you need so that you can press forward. You're keeping your faith from being contaminated because when you give God praise, you are "walk[ing] by faith, not by sight" (2 Corinthians 5:7). When you give God praise in spite of how you feel or what's happening around you, you put yourself in a seat of expectation! There's always blessings in return when you give God praise. Breakthrough takes place as you show God that, in spite of where you are, you still believe. You still trust Him, because you know it's by faith that circumstances will get better!

When you lack in giving God praise and worshiping Him in spirit and in truth, you give your feelings opportunity to contaminate your faith. You block moments to reflect on how good God has been to you and how good He'll always be in spite of tough times. Instead of allowing yourself to drown in your feelings and emotions, instead of allowing what you see and how you feel to deactivate your faith, you ought to praise God. With God, you'll never be disappointed, and greater is always ahead of you!

Family, your faith in and praise and worship to God add value to each other. They work together to create an environment that sets the atmosphere for God to dwell, in which healing, restoration, and deliverance take place!

This is why you can't allow your faith to be contaminated. God called you to be His ambassador, a game changer, a trend setter for the Kingdom of God. By faith, with the Word of God, you are called to change whatever needs to be changed in your community, on our job, in your house, in the midst of your family. Everywhere you go and in all that you do, God wants to meet your faith, with His power.

LACK OF FAITHFULNESS

You definitely can't keep your faith from being contaminated if you're not faithful.

Nobody has been or will be more faithful than God. Every day is an opportunity to make the choice to stay committed to God no matter what! We are called by God, the chosen of God, the elect of God, enriched by His grace to be in fellowship with our Lord and Savior Jesus Christ. The choice to remain faithful, stay committed, and keep trusting God in the midst of trials brings His blessings. Circumstances may be hard at times, but God is able to sustain, heal, deliver, restore, and protect us at all times. God is always with those who trust in Him through life's most difficult moments.

Lacking faithfulness to God and in your relationship with Him can contaminate your faith. When you lack faithfulness, you lack discipline. Not being faithful in what God called you to do can cause you to lose your focus. You become easily distracted, lacking in productivity, putting your life and what God has for you on pause. Not flowing the way God created you to flow is a blessing blocker. You will realize along the way that your faith has been contaminated.

Being faithful to God will sustain your faith, open doors for you, and position you for promotion and elevation. Being faithful will position you to be honored, because you become reliable. Others can depend on you, like your pastor, your boss, your family, your community, and more. You're in the flow of God when you are faithful. It's better to be in the flow of God than to be in a flow of your own or having no flow at all and being stagnant.

When we live according to God's Word, when we live and move by faith, we focus on our purpose and not our problems. When you're operating in your purpose consistently, worshiping God daily, you won't have time to focus on your problems. You won't have time to be doubtful or fearful or frustrated or sad or depressed or down, because your mind is always stayed on Jesus. You're able to continually do the work of the Lord whether in your home, community, church services, or on your job. You sustain a high quality of life when you are faithful, maintaining all that God has put in you. He freely provides your joy, peace, and happiness, sustaining the quality of life He created you to enjoy. These are Kingdom benefits. God promised and provides when we are faithful to Him, because being faithful is a Kingdom principle. God's Kingdom principles add healthy spiritual structure to our lives.

Faithfulness: to be firm in adherence to promises or in observance of duty.

The nature of God's faithfulness gives us peace of mind, confidence, and assurance that we are protected, safe, and secure in His care.

Your faith is contaminated when there is a lack of faithfulness because you are not consistent in the things of God. You are delaying your destiny instead of using your gifts, knowledge, skill set, and God-given abilities to add value to this world, your life, your family's lives, and the lives of those you'll connect with. Not being faithful can restrict your growth, putting limitations on how far God desires to take you. You can miss out on what God wants to reveal to you. You can literally block everything you're believing in God for, because there's no preparation in motion. To be faithful is also to prepare. You must always be learning, growing, planning, putting in the work, and advancing in the earth in God's way.

As children of God, it is important to be faithful to God. It is one thing to simply believe in Him and another to be faithful to Him. Faithfulness requires us to submit our ways to God. It comes from a place of realizing that we are in need of a Savior and that He is in control of our lives. True faithfulness to God shapes the way we live. For example, we are loyal in our relationships here on earth and truly love others.

1 Samuel 12:24 AMP
"Only fear the LORD [with awe and profound reverence] and serve Him faithfully with all your heart; for consider what great things He has done for you."

1 Corinthians 4:2 KJV
"Moreover it is required in stewards, that a man be found faithful."

Matthew 25:23 KJV
"His lord said unto him, Well done, good and faithful servant; thou hast been faithful over a few things, I will make thee ruler over many

things: enter thou into the joy of thy lord."

1 Corinthians 15:57-58 KJV
"But thanks be to God, which giveth us the victory through our Lord
Jesus Christ. Therefore, my beloved brethren, be ye stedfast, unmove-
able, always abounding in the work of the Lord, forasmuch as ye know
that your labour is not in vain in the Lord."

We ought to be faithful, because God is faithful! He always has been,
He is, and He always will be. To remain faithful is to be loyal, consistent, and steadfast. To remain faithful is to stay focused, and be
anchored in who God is and in His Word. Every day of our lives, we
must remain faithful to what God has declared in His Word and to
what He has created and purposed us to do. He has called us to the
positions we have and the areas we're blessed to serve in. God has
anointed us with gifts to manage well and called us to declare who He
is and speak His Word to the world!

It was God who planned long ago the redemption of mankind, before
the foundation of the world (1 Peter 1:20). By the grace of God
through faith in Christ, we have become the children of God and joint
heirs with our Lord and Savior Jesus Christ (Romans 8:16-17). God
has great plans for each and every one of us.

At times, we may act contrary to His plans and buck against them. We
may grumble and complain, but we must realize that God knows best.
God should always be the one in control of our lives. He knows what
tomorrow holds. He sees the future and therefore knows what is best
for us. Our purpose is to fulfill God's purpose. We were purchased by
Him with the blood of Christ.

1 Corinthians 6:20 KJV
"For ye are bought with a price: therefore glorify God in your body,
and in your spirit, which are God's."

We belong entirely to God. Because of this, we should honor God
through being faithful to Him, maintaining our focus, and remaining
pure in heart. We must fully live our lives for Christ, like Christ lived
for His Father. God knows what He's doing! Never doubt your purpose
or that you have a reason for being who you are, where you are. God
has a greater plan in mind concerning us. We just have to realize it and

surrender ourselves to His plan.

Family, be consistent in what God has called you to do, and God will move unexpectedly in your life. God honors consistency. Remain faithful to God, knowing He will always see you through.

Remain faithful to God, because God will always remain faithful to you. God has been faithful. God is faithful. And God will always be faithful.

Galatians 6:9 KJV
"And let us not be weary in well doing: for in due season we shall reap,
if we faint not."

My challenge to you is this: Think about the ways you show your faithfulness to God. Are there things that are getting in the way of being faithful? What areas of your life have you not given over to Him? Spend some time in prayer. Ask God to make these things clear to you, so that He can grow you in your faithfulness.

Being faithful to God gives us great peace and assurance that we will be brought through every storm. We know His promises of blessings and the reward of eternal life in Heaven. We can grow in our faithfulness by simply having a personal relationship with Christ. When we are truly faithful to Him and obey His commands (living by faith according to His Word), all that God has promised will be evident in our lives. Remain faithful, so that your faith will never become contaminated.

DISOBEDIENCE

Definition: Failure or refusal to obey rules or someone in authority; refusal to comply, or to disregard.

Family, out of everything we've gone over throughout this series, if there is anything that will contaminate your faith to the fullest, it's disobedience to God's Word and who He is. It is so disrespectful to disobey God when He loves us in so many ways. He looks out for us in ways we don't deserve, haven't earned, didn't ask for, and cannot fathom even in these present times. God's love for us and His grace and mercy and compassion toward us are eternally immeasurable. We should be obedient to God, so that our faith is not contaminated, simply because of who God is. His Word developed our faith in the first place. Remember, Family, the Word of the Lord:

Romans 10:17 KJV
"So then faith cometh by hearing, and hearing by the word of God."

Flowing in disobedience can not only contaminate your faith but also remove your faith. When you're not following the way of God, you're in God's way. When we disobey God, we are against Him. He asks us through His commandments in His Word to follow His way. When we disobey God, there are consequences. Family, we have to remember His commandments and rules are there to protect us.

If you're not living according to God's Word, following His instructions, there's a chance you don't believe in who He is and what He has promised in the first place. Family, this is why we have to take ownership of our faith, getting to know God for ourselves. You have to have an encounter with Him to know Him. You must have a life-changing experience with God in order to respond to Him, obeying His word and His voice. You cannot live the life God created you to live without faith. You cannot succeed in living the life God created you to live if you don't have His Word as your foundation. Without His Word, you will sink in difficult times because you literally have nothing firm on which to stand.

Lacking God's Word as your foundation and not following His way means your faith is not active. It's dead. This puts you in an extremely vulnerable position moving forward, because you're open to wrongful influence or attacks by spiritual wickedness. To survive, you must have God's Word and faith. You have to obey God!

Family, you have to maintain your faith. You have to allow Jesus to lead you. You have to live this life God's way. You have to be disciplined, "strong in the Lord, and in the power of his might" (Ephesians 6:10 KJV).

When you allow your faith to become contaminated by disobedience, you're allowing your feelings to lead you instead of following the Holy Spirit. I've shared with you before in this series that when you're in your feelings, you're not in faith. Faith and your feelings can't coexist.

The enemy wants you to be in your feelings and tries to keep you there. When you allow him to have space in your life, you cannot move in faith and obey God's Word.

Family, you can't afford to have your faith contaminated! You have to trust God, love Him with your whole heart, be obedient, and know that His intentions towards you are always good! God has given us the blueprint in Deuteronomy 28 on how to succeed and live a blessed life. He shows us how to overcome, experience His goodness, and be restored and made whole. God lets us know that obedience brings blessings and disobedience brings curses. You ought to want the blessings of the Lord, because:

Proverbs 10:22 KJV
"The blessing of the LORD, it maketh rich, and he addeth no sorrow with it."

The blessings of the Lord are help and approval from God stamped upon your life. This means you will succeed in whatever He has assigned you to do. We are joint heirs of Jesus Christ. Whatever trials may come your way, God's blessings will cause you to come out better than where you were before.

Deuteronomy 28:1-14 NLT
"'If you fully obey the Lord your God and carefully keep all his commands that I am giving you today, the Lord your God will set you high above all the nations of the world. You will experience all these blessings if you obey the Lord your God:
"'Your towns and your fields will be blessed. Your children and your crops will be blessed. The offspring of your herds and flocks will be blessed. Your fruit baskets and breadboards will be blessed. Wherever you go and whatever you do, you will be blessed.
"'The Lord will conquer your enemies when they attack you. They will attack you from one direction, but they will scatter from you in seven!
"'The Lord will guarantee a blessing on everything you do and will fill your storehouses with grain. The Lord your God will bless you in the land he is giving you.
"'If you obey the commands of the Lord your God and walk in his ways, the Lord will establish you as his holy people as he swore he would do. Then all the nations of the world will see that you are a

people claimed by the Lord, and they will stand in awe of you. "'The Lord will give you prosperity in the land he swore to your ancestors to give you, blessing you with many children, numerous livestock, and abundant crops. The Lord will send rain at the proper time from his rich treasury in the heavens and will bless all the work you do. You will lend to many nations, but you will never need to borrow from them. If you listen to these commands of the Lord your God that I am giving you today, and if you carefully obey them, the Lord will make you the head and not the tail, and you will always be on top and never at the bottom. You must not turn away from any of the commands I am giving you today, nor follow after other gods and worship them.'"

Remember, "the blessing of the LORD, it maketh rich, and he addeth no sorrow with it" (Proverbs 10:22 KJV). As you press toward a new year, know that everything God adds to your life is always for your good. What God adds to your life is always for your benefit and betterment. What God adds to your life is for your health and prosperity. What God adds to your life is for you to use to add value to this world.

None of this can happen if you are not in faith and being obedient to God. God wants to work through you! He desires to advance His Kingdom in the earth. You are dearly loved, completely accepted, totally forgiven, and uniquely chosen by God. He wants to do a greater work through you. As you lift up the name of Jesus, He'll draw all unto Himself to save, to heal, to deliver, to set free. We have to submit to the will of God, because it's not about you and it's not about me—it's all about Jesus! God will bless you to reap the benefits along the way.

By faith, prepare, get in alignment with God and His Word, be obedient to Him, stay in faith and out of your feelings, and you'll receive the blessings of the Lord. Things are about to get better for you, if you believe it. Move by faith and you shall receive it, in Jesus' Mighty Name. Remain faithful, so that your faith will never become contaminated.

#ByFaithWeGood

From Faith To Faith

Family, there's a reason God gave me Romans 1:16-17 as the theme scripture for this series. There should never be a time in our life where it's okay to not be in faith.

Romans 1:16-17 KJV
"For I am not ashamed of the gospel of Christ: for it is the power of God unto salvation to every one that believeth; to the Jew first, and also to the Greek. For therein is the righteousness of God revealed from faith to faith: as it is written, The just shall live by faith."

We're created to go from faith to faith. God takes us from faith to faith. We're created to live from faith to faith. From the beginning to the end, from start to finish.

When you accept Jesus and your Lord and Savior, Jesus saves you. He raises you. He heals you. He makes you whole. As He promised, Jesus fills you with the Holy Ghost. We cannot be ashamed of loving God, serving God, trusting God, and committing our lives to being in and maintaining a personal relationship with Him.

Jesus did everything by faith. Every area of our lives is to be lived by faith. We live by faith not just in our lives as Christians, but in our business lives, our family lives, and our recreational lives. Every area of our lives is to be lived by faith. To live by faith, it is having faith from start to finish. Faith to faith even means we've got to grow in faith.

With God, everything is by faith. All we have to do is BELIEVE!

We accept Jesus Christ (have a personal relationship with Him) by FAITH.

We bring God's Word to life by speaking it by FAITH.

Everything in God's kingdom is done by FAITH.

Everything God does through us is done by FAITH.

Everything we receive from God is received by FAITH.

We make every one of our requests known to God by FAITH.

Having strong faith is having complete trust and confidence in God. It is strongly believing in God and who He is and in His Word! Through strong faith in God and His Word, we'll be equipped and positioned with a strong foundation to "walk by faith, not by sight" (2 Corinthians 5:7).

We overcome by faith. Every obstacle that comes our way, no matter what the enemy tries—with God by faith, we always win. We can accomplish the goals we set out to accomplish. We can be who God created us to be. We can go where God says we can go. We can do what God created us to do. Living by faith in God and in His Word, you'll always have all you need. You're covered by God's divine protection. You can walk in the favor of God ordained for your life. You never have to live fearfully or in worry. You can be as great as God created you to be. You are secure in Him.

Living by faith is allowing the Holy Spirit to guide you through all the days of your life. It is being renewed in spirit and in your mind. It is allowing the Spirit of God to transcend your whole life and everything that connects you to Him.

Never be ashamed of the Word of God, for it is the power of God at work in you, bringing salvation to everyone who believes. God's Word has power and there's power in trusting God's Word. There's power in being unashamed, sharing and declaring God's Word.

The Word of God has been given to us as a guide and a directive as to how we should live. No man can add to it. None of us can save ourselves. God alone has the capacity and ability to save. God alone has the power to redeem! It is through belief in the gospel of Christ—which is the death, burial, and resurrection of the Lord Jesus Christ alone—that we are saved.

When you get into the Word of God and let the Word of God get in you, you'll never lose or fail. You will always win! Never be ashamed. Instead, always stand firm on the Word of the Lord.

James 1:2-4 NLT
"Dear brothers and sisters, when troubles of any kind come your way, consider it an opportunity for great joy. For you know that when your faith is tested, your endurance has a chance to grow. So let it grow, for when your endurance is fully developed, you will be perfect and complete, needing nothing."

When tough times come your way, it's a time for great joy because you have an opportunity to develop. It is time to establish your faith in God's ability to bring you out. God is giving your endurance a chance to grow, so that you can remain strong and press forward victoriously. Being perfect and complete means you are established in who you are in Christ. You need nothing because God is your source, and He provides all that you need in abundance.

Psalm 92:13-15 KJV
"Those that be planted in the house of the LORD shall flourish in the courts of our God. They shall still bring forth fruit in old age; they shall be fat and flourishing; To shew that the Lord is upright: he is my rock, and there is no unrighteousness in him."

Have you ever noticed that when you plant something in the ground, it grows where you planted it? Once a seed is planted in good soil, you water it and allow it to be nurtured by the sun. Over time, that seed begins to grow.

In the same way, Family, God has given us life with a purpose. We are to bear good fruit for others and contribute something good in helping others. We are to add value to this world, bringing Heaven to earth and advancing God's Kingdom. God's plan is perfect.

We are meant to grow where God plants us, remaining in faith and going from faith to faith. You cannot allow anything to interfere with your faith.

We can't afford to be out of faith.

You will always flourish, prosper, and grow when you are planted in the foundation of who God is, His Word, and His will for your life!

Psalm 92:13 KJV

"Those that be planted in the house of the Lord shall flourish in the courts of our God."

To flourish is to grow, to thrive, to achieve and succeed, and to prosper. You can grow and live in this way in your life with God. To be planted is to be deeply rooted, established, in position. We flourish when we align ourselves with God's plan for our lives. We must align ourselves to God's Word and take ownership of our true identity in Christ, giving birth to our full God-given potential.

God wants us to flourish as He cares for us. He gives us everything we need to flourish as His children. With God, there's never a need to worry. You will always prosper when you let God lead you. When you believe God is your source, all will be well.

We have to stay focused and faith-filled, moving from faith to faith. We must get in position, stay in position, and own our position in Christ Jesus.

Hebrews 11:1 KJV

"Now faith is the substance of things hoped for, the evidence of things not seen."

Faith is being sure of what you hope for and certain of what you do not see. **What is faith?** Faith is being fully assured. Faith is the formula for the manifestation of God's Word. It is not wavering or doubting at all. Faith is getting an understanding of God's Word and knowing how to apply it to your life in every situation that comes your way. Faith is knowing how to put faith to work: speaking the Word of God. What you speak and believe, you shall receive.

Faith sees the invisible, believes the unbelievable, and receives the impossible. All we have to do is BELIEVE! With God, FAITH is mandatory.

Remember, Family, God has been faithful. God is faithful. And God will always be faithful. God will always work out every situation for your good! Let Jesus lead you. Stay focused, and always press forward by faith. Remain faithful, so that your faith will never become contaminated!

#ByFaithWeGood

"For We Walk By Faith, Not By Sight"
2 Corinthians 5:7 KJV

IT'S YOUR TIME
"Extending The Invitation"

Romans 10:9 KJV
"That if thou shalt confess with thy mouth the Lord Jesus, and shalt believe in thine heart that God hath raised him from the dead, thou shalt be saved."

As you've been reading this book, perhaps these words have spoken to you in a special way. With all that you've read, you now want to receive and experience who God is for yourself. You want to position yourself to "[cast] all your care upon him; for he careth for you" (1 Peter 5:7 KJV).

I encourage to accept Jesus Christ into your life as your Lord and Savior. Falling in love with Jesus is the best thing that has ever happened to me. When you accept Christ into your life, you'll also be a witness that falling in love with Jesus is the best thing that's ever happened to you! God freely adopts us into His eternal family. I encourage you to open up your heart today, and invite Jesus into your life and into all of your circumstances.

If the person I'm speaking to is you, repeat this prayer:

Father, forgive me, for I have sinned and fallen short of Your glory.
I believe that Jesus Christ is the Son of God.
I believe that Jesus Christ died for my sins.
I believe that Jesus Christ rose with all power.
I believe that Jesus Christ is so real and so alive.
Jesus, save me. I accept you as my Lord and Savior. Come into my heart. Come into my life, and stay in my life.
Holy Spirit, come into my heart. Come into my life and stay in my life. Have your way, so that I live according to God's Word, His will, and His way.
In Jesus' Name, Amen!

Family, if you fully believe in the prayer you just declared, you just got saved! This day will be the start and new beginning of the best days of the rest of your life.

Your time for greater is now. Stay focused, and always press forward by faith!

#ByFaithWeGood

Conclusion

Family, thank you so much for your support and for taking the time to read this book. I pray that you are inspired and encouraged to be consistent in the way God created you to live and function in the earth, always pressing forward by faith!

I'm forever grateful for how God used me to lift Him up and to encourage and pray for you all throughout this devotional. It is all for His glory! I pray that every word has truly been a blessing to you. As you press forward, I will continue to encourage and pray for you as God allows. It is not about us, but it is and always will be all about Jesus. His will. His way. His plan. His purpose. His desire. Let us seek what God wants more than what we want, looking forward to all that God is going to do through and for us in the years to come.

Ephesians 3:17-19 KJV
"That Christ may dwell in your hearts by faith; that ye, being rooted and grounded in love, May be able to comprehend with all saints what is the breadth, and length, and depth, and height; And to know the love of Christ, which passeth knowledge, that ye might be filled with all the fulness of God."

I pray that out of God's glorious riches He will strengthen you with power through His Spirit in your inner being, so that Christ may dwell in your hearts through faith. I pray that you, being rooted and established in love, may have power, together with all the Lord's holy people, to grasp how wide and long and high and deep the love of Christ is (Ephesians 3:16-18 NLT). I pray that you may know God's love that surpasses knowledge—that you may be filled to the measure of all the fullness of God.

God is always with you.

He'll always have you covered.
God is always able.

Things are about to get better for you in Jesus' Mighty Name.

Let Jesus lead you.

Stay focused and always press forward by faith!

#ByFaithWeGood

About The Author

Minister Bernard Marrow is a native of Philadelphia, Pennsylvania. Currently living in the State of Illinois, he is the founder and president of By Faith We Good Ministry Inc.

Minister Bernard Marrow is a singer, songwriter, and musician. He is a faithful, dedicated hard worker who was ordained as a Deacon on June 18th, 2011, received his ministerial license on April 27th, 2014 under the leadership of Pastor Robert T. Moore Jr. He currently resides in Chicago, Illinois with his beautiful wife, Vanessa where he was relicensed as a minister at Empowered People Church, a ministry under Kingdom Church International Ministries, on January 9, 2022 under the leadership of Pastors Drs. John & Kisia Coleman Overseer & Lead Pastor.

Through the leading of the Holy Spirit, Minister Bernard has provided this book as a resource for believers to use everyday to help them stay focused and grounded in who God is and His Word. He encourages believers to always press forward by faith. Minister Bernard Marrow is a man of prayer, very passionate about the purpose God assigned to his life. He focuses on equipping others to be strong in their faith, always grounded in God's Word and advancing God's Kingdom!

Why? Because ByFaithWeGood!

"For We Walk By Faith, Not By Sight"
2 Corinthians 5:7 KJV

Connect with
The Author

Minister Bernard On Facebook: **Min Bernard Marrow**
ByFaithWeGood on Facebook: **By Faith We Good Ministry Inc.**

Instagram: **@min.marrow**
ByFaithWeGood Instagram: **@bfwgministry**

Snapchat: Min. Marrow

Twitter: **@MinMarrow**
ByFaithWeGood Twitter: **@ByFaithWeGood**

Email:
Min. Bernard Marrow:
connectwithmin.marrow@gmail.com

ByFaithWeGood:
info@bfwgministry.com

Website:
www.BFWGMinistry.com
www.ShopBFWG.com